Sexual Healing

A Spiritual Guide to Breaking Generational Cycles and Reclaiming Your Authority

Esaias Merritt

SEXUAL HEALING: A Spiritual Guide to Breaking Generational Cycles and Reclaiming Your Authority

ISBN: 979-8-90417-011-0

ISBN: 979-8-90417-018-9 (Hardback)

First Edition

Published by Merritt International Publisher, Grovetown, GA - www.bspmerritt.org

Printed in the United States of America

Contents

Foreword

By a Husband and Wife Married 49 Years

After forty-nine years of marriage, we have learned a few things, not from theory, not from trends, but from time, tears, triumphs, and the tender mercy of God. We have watched culture shift like sand beneath the feet of generations. We have seen what was once whispered become celebrated, what was once sacred become casual, and what God designed as holy become distorted by a world determined to redefine truth.

It is from that vantage point that we write this foreword.

This book, *Sexual Healing* by Esaias Meritt, is not merely a commentary on sexuality, it is an unveiling. It pulls back the curtain on what the author calls the "55s", the lies, ideologies, and narratives embedded within modern media, music, and culture that are not accidental, but intentional. Strategic. Engineered. These lies are not random missteps of society; they are carefully crafted messages designed to shape desire, distort identity, and ultimately groom the soul for bondage.

We have lived long enough to recognize patterns. What this book names as a "con" is real. And it is gendered. Men are deceived one way; women another. Each is targeted uniquely, but both are led toward the same destination, disconnection from God's design and entanglement in counterfeit intimacy.

What makes this work especially profound is that it does not stop at exposure, it moves into explanation. The author introduces a framework that is both ancient in truth and fresh in articulation: the distinction between the *Asa*, the physical body, and the *Bara*, the spiritual essence. For decades, we have counseled couples who tried to solve spiritual wounds with physical solutions. This book explains why that never works. You cannot heal the *Bara* with what only touches the *Asa*.

And here is where the message deepens.

In a culture that reduces sex to biology or emotion, this book restores its true weight. Sex is not merely an act. It is not just connection. It is covenant. It is, as the author so powerfully describes, a *blood covenant*, a portal, a spiritual welding, where two lives are fused in ways far beyond what the eye can see or the mind can fully comprehend.

We wish someone had explained it this clearly to our generation.

Yet this is not a book of condemnation, it is a book of invitation.

Perhaps one of the most moving sections is the journey through the life of the woman at the well. Her story is not treated as a distant biblical account, but as a mirror held up to every searching soul. Six relationships. Six attempts at fulfillment. Six wells that ran dry. And then, the seventh Man. Not just another man, but the Messiah. The One who does not take from her but restores her. The One who does not use her but reveals her. The One who does not bind her but frees her. We have seen that transformation in real life.

Over the years, we have walked with individuals and couples whose lives were tangled in regret, shame, and broken intimacy. And we have witnessed the same truth this book proclaims: no human relationship can heal what only Christ can restore.

The closing movement of this book is as courageous as it is necessary. Healing requires leaving. It requires the willingness to walk through a wilderness season, where old attachments are severed, false identities are stripped away, and the soul is recalibrated in the presence of God. The concept of a "spiritual bill of divorcement" is not merely poetic—it is prophetic. It speaks to the authority believers have to renounce every ungodly covenant and reclaim the wholeness that was always God's intent.

After nearly five decades of marriage, we can say this with conviction: healing is possible. Purity is not outdated. Covenant still matters. And God is still in the business of restoring what culture has tried to ruin.

This book will challenge you. It may confront areas you have avoided. It will certainly call you higher. But if you allow it, it will also guide you toward freedom.

We commend this work not only for what it reveals, but for where it leads.

May you read it with an open heart.

May you wrestle with its truths.

And may you, like the woman at the well, encounter the One who finally satisfies.

With enduring love and tested faith,

Bishop Dr. Jake Givan, Jr. and Elder Deborah J. Givan

A Husband and Wife, 49 Years Married

Prologue: The Seventh Man Encounter

You are carrying something that was never meant to be yours.

Maybe it's the weight of a relationship that ended years ago but still whispers your name in the quiet moments. Maybe it's a shame that wraps around your chest every time you look in the mirror, reminding you of every compromise, every moment you gave yourself away, every time you said yes when your spirit screamed no. Maybe it's the exhaustion of trying to build something new while dragging the wreckage of the past behind you like chains you can't see but can always feel.

You've tried to move forward. You've prayed. You've repented. You've promised God and yourself that this time would be different. But somehow, the same patterns keep showing up. The same type of person. The same kind of pain. The same cycle of hope and heartbreak, connection and collapse, intimacy and isolation.

And the question that haunts you in the middle of the night is this: *Why can't I break free?*

Let me tell you something that might change everything: You are not broken. You are bound.

There is a difference.

Broken things need to be fixed. Bound things need to be *loosed*. And what has you bound is not a character flaw, not a lack of willpower, not even a pattern of bad decisions; though those may be symptoms. What has you bound is something far more ancient, far more intentional, and far more spiritual than you've been taught to recognize.

You are bound by covenant.

Not the kind of covenant you made at an altar in a church. The kind of covenant you make in a bedroom. In a car. In a moment of longing, loneliness, or lust. The kind of covenant that was sealed not with a ring, but with your body. Not with vows spoken aloud, but with a merging of souls that you didn't even know was happening.

And here's what no one told you: every sexual encounter is a blood covenant. Every time you give your body to someone, you are opening a portal between your spirit and theirs. You are not just "having sex." You are fusing. Merging. Creating a spiritual bond that doesn't dissolve just because the relationship ends.

The world told you it was casual. The culture told you it was empowering. The enemy told you it didn't matter. But your soul knows the truth. Your soul has been screaming it for years. You feel it in the exhaustion. In the shame. In the way you can't seem to shake the presence of people who are no longer in your life. In the way their voices still echo in your mind, their patterns still show up in your choices, their trauma still lives in your body.

You are not imagining it. You are not being dramatic. You are not "too sensitive" or "too spiritual." You are experiencing the very real, very tangible consequences of unholy soul ties; covenants that were never sanctioned by God but are binding, nonetheless.

And until you understand the mechanics of what happened, you will never be able to break free.

The Woman at the Well

There is a woman in the Gospel of John, chapter 4, who understood this better than most. She is known simply as "the Woman at the Well," and her story is the framework for everything you are about to read in this book.

When Jesus met her, she had been married five times. Five

legal, socially recognized marriages. Five men who had the legal right to her body, her name, her future. Five covenants that ended, whether through death, divorce, or abandonment, we don't know. But we do know this: she was currently living with a sixth man who was *not* her husband.

Five husbands. One current partner. Six soul ties. Six open portals. Six voices in her head. Six patterns overlapping in her soul.

And Jesus, in His infinite mercy and surgical precision, looked at her and said: *"Go, call thy husband."*

He wasn't cruel. He was *diagnostic*. He was naming the thing that had her bound. He was identifying the root of her shame, her isolation, her thirst that no amount of water could satisfy. He was pointing to the covenants; the legal agreements, the spiritual bonds, the soul ties that were still active, still speaking, still shaping her identity.

And here's the part that will set you free: Jesus didn't condemn her. He offered her living water.

He didn't say, "You're too broken." He didn't say, "You've made too many mistakes." He didn't say, "You need to clean yourself up before you can come to Me." He said, *"If you drink of the water I give you, you will never thirst again."*

He was offering her something the five husbands couldn't give. Something the current man couldn't provide. Something no human being, no matter how good or how loving, could ever supply.

He was offering her the Seventh Man.

The Seventh Man

The number seven in Scripture represents completion. Perfection. Divine order. And to understand the power of the Seventh Man, you must first understand what the first six represent, and why they will always leave you empty.

The Five Men represent the broken, incomplete human attempts at covenant. These are the relationships that opened portals you didn't know existed. The marriages that ended. The commitments that failed. The people who had legal, social, or emotional access to your body and your soul, and left pieces of themselves behind when they walked away. These five created soul ties, the voices, the patterns that still echo in your mind. They are your history. Your trauma. Your unhealed wounds. And no matter how hard you try to "move on," their presence lingers because the covenants were never properly severed.

But here's what most people miss: the sixth man is not another person. The sixth man is the cycle itself.

The Sixth Man is the pattern you fall into when you try to fill a God-shaped void with human connection. He is the counterfeit intimacy that *looks* like love but has no covenant, no commitment, no authority to heal. He is what happens when you take what doesn't belong to you, or give what you were never meant to give, because the hunger is so deep, the loneliness so suffocating, that you convince yourself *this time* will be different.

The sixth man is the endless placeholder: longing, connection, temporary relief, emptiness, shame, and back to longing. He is the relationship that feels like it's filling the void but is actually just numbing the pain or going through the motions. He is the person you're with right now, not because they're "the one," but because you can't bear to be alone with the voices of the first five. He is the cycle of trying to be your own savior, your own healer, your own source, and failing every single time.

The sixth man is you, trying to do for yourself what only God can do. He is the illusion that if you just find the *right person*, the *right* connection, the *right* experience, you will finally feel whole. But you won't. Because the sixth man is not a solution, he is a symptom. He is proof that you are trying to satisfy spiritual hunger with physical connection. He is the evidence that you are drawing from a cistern instead of drinking from the well.

And here's the devastating truth: you can leave the first five and still be trapped by the sixth. You can cut off every toxic relationship, block every number, delete every photo, and still find yourself in the same cycle with a different face. Because the sixth man is not about *who* you're with. It's about *what you're seeking*. And what you're seeking is something no human being can provide.

This is why the Woman at the Well kept coming back to the cistern. This is why she had five husbands and was living with a sixth man. She wasn't looking for love; she was looking for *life*. She was trying to fill a void that only God could fill. And every time a relationship ended, every time a man walked away, every time the temporary relief wore off, she went back to the well. Back to the cycle. Back to the sixth man.

Until Jesus showed up.

The Seventh Man is Jesus Christ. He is not another attempt. He is not another relationship. He is not another person who *might* be able to heal you if you just try hard enough. He is the *only* One who can take what the first five created and restore it. The *only* One who can break the cycle of the sixth man and fill the void that has been driving you into bondage. The *only* One who can close the portals that were opened without permission, silence the voices that have been tormenting you, and make you *new*, not improved, not recovered, but *new*. A New Creation. *Bara*, not *Asa*.

The Seventh Man is the completion. The perfection. The divine order that the first six could never provide. He is the living water that satisfies the thirst so completely that you never have to go back to the cistern again. He is the One who meets you in the shame, in the mess, in the middle of the cycle, and says, *"I know everything you've ever done. And I'm offering you life anyway."*

This is why the number seven matters. The first five were covenants that failed. The sixth man is the cycle of trying to save yourself. But the Seventh Man is the Savior. He is the One who doesn't just heal the wounds, He *becomes* the source. He doesn't just close the portals; He *fills* the void. He doesn't just break the cycle; He *replaces* it with something eternal.

And here's the most important part: you cannot break free from the sixth man without encountering the Seventh Man. You can leave relationships. You can change your environment. You can swear off dating, delete the apps, commit to celibacy. But if you don't allow Jesus to fill the void that the sixth man represents, you will always go back. Because the sixth man is not a person, he is a hunger. And that hunger will not go away until it is satisfied by the only One who can truly satisfy it.

This is not a book about "getting over" your past. This is not a book about "moving on" or "letting go" or any other passive, powerless language that the world uses to describe healing. This is a book about spiritual warfare. About authority. About understanding the mechanics of the soul so that you can take back what was stolen, renounce what was never yours, and step into the identity that God has been holding for you since before you were born.

This is a book about covenant, how it works, how it binds, and how it can be broken.

This is a book about portals, what they are, how they open, and how to close them.

This is a book about frequency, the spiritual atmosphere you create with your words, your thoughts, your rituals, and your agreements.

This is a book about the voices, the mother of Shame, the Father of Lust, the Ancestral Altar, and the Current Man; and how to silence them so you can finally hear the voice of the Seventh Man.

And most importantly, this is a book about you, not the version of you that shame says you are (*asa*), but the version of you that God created you to be (*bara*). The you that exists beyond the trauma, beyond the mistakes, beyond the covenants that were never meant to define you. The you that can finally stop running to the sixth man because you have encountered the Seventh.

What This Book Is and What It Isn't

Let me be clear about what you're holding in your hands.

This is not therapy. Therapy is valuable, and I encourage you to seek it if you need it. But this book is not about processing emotions or unpacking childhood wounds, though those things may come up along the way.

This is not psychology. Psychology can help you understand *why* you do what you do. But this book is about the *spiritual mechanics* behind what you do, the unseen forces, the covenants, the portals, the frequencies that shape your choices before you even make them.

This is not self-help. Self-help assumes that you have the

power within yourself to fix what's broken. But you don't. You can't. No amount of positive thinking, vision boards, or affirmations will close a portal that was opened through blood covenant. Only the blood of Jesus can do that.

This is spiritual warfare. This is deliverance. This is restoration.

And it requires you to do something that might feel uncomfortable, even terrifying: you have to face the truth. You have to name the covenants. You have to acknowledge the portals. You have to confront the voices. You have to stop running from the Wilderness and start walking through it, because the Wilderness is not punishment, it's preparation. It's the place where God strips away everything that isn't Him so that you can finally see who you really are.

The Journey Ahead

This book is divided into three parts, and each part corresponds to a stage of your healing journey.

Part I: The Theology of the Portal will teach you the mechanics. You'll learn about *asa* versus *bara*, the difference between who shame says you are and who God created you to be. You'll learn about blood covenant, soul ties, and the spiritual reality of sex. You'll learn about the voices, the Mother of Shame, the Father of Lust, the Ancestral Altar, and the Current Man, and how they work together to keep you bound. And you'll meet the Woman at the Well, whose story will become your roadmap.

Part II: The Diagnosis of the Soul will teach you how to identify what needs to be healed. You'll learn the Art of Leaving, how to sever unholy soul ties and renounce covenants that were never sanctioned by God. You'll learn the Power of Cleaving, how to prepare yourself for sacred fusion with the right person at the right time. And you'll learn the Ritual of the Soul, how to replace Death Rituals (the patterns that lead you back into bondage) with Life Rituals (the practices that keep you free).

Part III: The Pathway to Restoration will teach you how to build the Altar, how to take your story of shame and transform it into a weapon of warfare. You'll learn how to walk in the authority of a New Creation, how to shift the frequency of your life, and how to establish a generational legacy of blessing instead of curse.

And then, for 30 days, you will *practice*. The workbook at the end of this book is not optional. It is not a "bonus" or a "supplement." It is the *application* of everything you've learned. It is where the theology becomes transformation. It is where knowledge becomes power.

Each day, you will do four things:

1. Read a Truth that counters the lie you've been believing.
2. Speak a Liturgy that shifts the frequency of your soul.
3. Declare Your Authority over the portals, the voices, and the covenants.
4. Practice a Ritual that establishes the new pattern.

This is not passive reading. This is active warfare. And by the end of 30 days, you will not be the same person you were when you started.

Why Now?

You might be wondering: *Why is this happening now? Why am I reading this book at this moment in my life?*

Here's what I believe: God is calling you out of the cistern.

The Woman at the Well was drawing water from a cistern, a man-made well that could only hold what was poured into it. It was stagnant. Limited. Dependent on human effort. And Jesus said to her, *"If you drink of this water, you will thirst again. But if you drink of the water I give you, it will become a well of water springing up into everlasting life."*

You have been drinking from cisterns. Relationships that couldn't hold what you needed. Patterns that couldn't sustain you. Covenants that couldn't heal you. And you keep coming back, over and over, hoping that *this time* it will be different. Hoping that *this person* will finally fill the void. Hoping that *this experience* will finally satisfy the thirst.

But it won't. It can't. Because cisterns were never meant to be your source.

God is calling you to the *well*, the place where living water flows, where healing is not a transaction but a transformation, where you don't have to keep coming back because the water He gives you becomes a *spring* inside of you. A source. A fountain. A portal of blessing instead of a portal of bondage.

And the reason it's happening now is because you're finally ready. You're tired of the cisterns. You're tired of the shame. You're tired of the cycles. You're ready to face the truth, to do the work, to walk through the Wilderness, and to meet the Seventh Man on the other side.

A Word Before You Begin

This journey will not be easy. There will be moments when

you want to close this book and walk away. There will be moments when the truth feels too heavy, the shame feels too loud, the Wilderness feels too long. There will be moments when you wonder if freedom is even possible for someone like you.

In those moments, I want you to remember this: Jesus met the Woman at the Well in the middle of the day, in the heat of the sun, when no one else was around. He didn't wait for her to clean herself up. He didn't wait for her to "get it together." He didn't wait for her to be "ready." He met her *where she was*, in the mess, in the shame, in isolation.

And He is meeting you here. Right now. In this moment. In this book. In this season of your life.

You are not too broken. You are not too far gone. You are not beyond the reach of the Seventh Man.

You are *exactly* where you need to be.

So take a breath. Say a prayer. And turn the page.

The Woman at the Well walked away from that encounter and became the first evangelist in the Gospel of John. She ran back to her city and said, *"Come, see a man who told me everything I ever did. Could this be the Christ?"*

Her shame became her testimony. Her bondage became her

breakthrough. Her story became a weapon.

And so will yours.

Welcome to *Sexual Healing*. Welcome to the journey from cistern to well, from bondage to freedom, from *asa* to *bara*.

Welcome to the rest of your life.

~ Esaias Merritt

PART I: THEOLOGY OF THE PORTAL

Chapter 1
The Hyper-Sexual Delusion:

Unmasking the Subtle Influence on the Modern Soul

Chapter 1: The Hyper-Sexual Delusion:

Unmasking the Subtle Influence on the Modern Soul

In a world where intimacy is celebrated yet simultaneously shrouded in stigma, the landscape of our souls has become a battlefield. Statistics tell a staggering story: nearly 40% of men and 30% of women grapple with sexual dysfunction. Globally, 1 in 6 individuals is suffering in silence. But these aren't just clinical numbers; they are the fruit of a profound spiritual miseducation. We have accepted a distorted perception of sex that disregards the purity of intimacy and leads us down a path of spiritual defilement.

The 55 Factor: How the World Cons You

I am reminded of the film Focus, where Will Smith plays a savvy con artist. In one pivotal scene at the Super Bowl, he wins a massive $2.4 million bet by "guessing" a specific number. His secret? He didn't guess. He had spent the entire day subtly "planting" that number in his mark's subconscious; on billboards, in the lobby, and even on the lapels of passersby.

Our society operates on the same principle. We are being told what to think about sex before we even realize we are thinking it. We live in a hyper-sexual culture where imagery is inescapable; from the $14 billion porn industry to the billboards we pass on our daily commute. Like the mark in the movie, we think we are making "free choices," but we are often just reacting to the "55s" the world has planted in our minds.

The Digital "55s": How Modern Media Plants Sexual Ideology

The con is more sophisticated now than ever. In Will Smith's film, the mark had to physically walk through a lobby, past billboards, and through crowds wearing numbered jerseys. Today, the "55s" come to you. They follow you. They learn your patterns, your weaknesses, your late-night vulnerabilities.

Consider the algorithm. You open Instagram at 11 PM, just scrolling to "unwind." Within three swipes, you encounter a fitness influencer in minimal clothing, a meme sexualizing a TV character, and an ad for lingerie you never searched for. The algorithm didn't guess what you wanted to see; it planted what you would want next. It studied your pause time, your scroll speed, and your engagement patterns. It knows you better than you know yourself.

TikTok operates on the same principle, but faster. The "For You" page is a masterclass in subconscious conditioning. A 15-second video normalizes casual hookup culture. Another glorifies "situationships." Another makes celibacy look like deprivation rather than devotion. You don't even have time to process one message before the next one loads. The "55s" aren't on billboards anymore; they're in your hand, refreshing every three seconds.

Dating apps have gamified intimacy itself. Tinder, Bumble, Hinge; they've turned human connection into a slot machine. Swipe. Swipe. Match. Dopamine hit. The apps aren't designed to help you find a covenant partner; they're designed to keep you swiping. The business model depends on you not finding lasting connection. Every profile picture is a "55." Every bio is a "55." Every "like" you receive whispers, this is what intimacy looks like now.

Then there's OnlyFans and the normalization of commodified sexuality. What was once hidden in the shadows of pornography is now celebrated as "empowerment" and "entrepreneurship." The message isn't just that sex can be bought, it's that sex should be monetized, that your body is your most valuable asset, that intimacy is a product to be marketed. The "55" here is insidious: Your worth is in your desirability. Your power is in your ability to be consumed.

Streaming platforms plant their own "55s" with surgical precision. Netflix autoplay takes you from a family comedy to a series where infidelity is normalized, where casual sex has no consequences, and where covenant marriage is portrayed as boring or oppressive. You didn't choose to watch that scene; it was three episodes deep into a show you were already invested in. The "55" was planted in episode one; you just didn't notice until episode six, when you were desensitized enough to accept it.

Even the music streaming through your earbuds is planting seeds. The top 40 hits aren't just catchy: they're theological statements about the nature of sex, love, and human connection. "We found love in a hopeless place." "I don't want to be your friend; I want to kiss your lips." "These hoes ain't loyal." Every hook, every chorus, every beat drop is a "55" being embedded into your subconscious soundtrack.

The cumulative effect is staggering. By the time you're an adult, you've been exposed to hundreds of thousands of sexual images and messages, most of which you never consciously chose to consume. You think you're making independent decisions about your sexuality, but you're actually just responding to the "55s" that have been planted since childhood. The world has been whispering a definition of sex into your ear for decades, and now, when you think about intimacy, you hear that whisper as if it were your own voice.

This is the con. You think you're free, but you've been set up.

The Gendered Trap: How the "55s" Target Men and Women Differently

The con artist knows his marks. He doesn't use the same approach on everyone; he tailors the con to the vulnerability. The hyper-sexual delusion operates the same way. It doesn't plant the same "55s" in men and women; it customizes the lie to exploit gender-specific insecurities.

For men, the "55s" whisper a relentless message: You are what you perform. Pornography doesn't just offer visual stimulation; it offers a script. It tells you what sex should look like, how long it should last, what your partner should look like, how they should respond. It creates a standard that no real human interaction can match. The result? Men enter real intimacy with a mental script written by an industry that profits from their inadequacy. They compare themselves to pixels. They measure their manhood by a standard designed to make them feel insufficient.

The "55s" for men also glorify conquest. Body count becomes a badge of honor. Virginity becomes something to "lose" rather than something to steward. Every movie, every locker room conversation, every rap lyric plants the same message: Real men consume. Real men conquer. Real men don't commit; they collect. And so, men enter relationships not as covenant partners but as consumers, not as protectors but as predators, not seeking to give but to take.

The addiction pathways are real. Neuroscience confirms what Scripture has always known: what you behold, you become. The dopamine cycle created by pornography mirrors the cycle of drug addiction. The brain rewires itself. The threshold for arousal increases. What once satisfied no longer does. The "55s" planted in adolescence become strongholds in adulthood, and men find themselves enslaved to appetites they never consciously chose to develop.

For women, the "55s" whisper a different lie: You are what you offer. The message isn't about performance, it's about desirability. Social media has turned every woman into a brand, every selfie into a product launch, every outfit into a marketing campaign. The "55s" tell women that their value is in their ability to be wanted, that their power is in their sex appeal, that their worth is measured in likes, follows, and male attention.

The body image warfare is relentless. Every Instagram model, every magazine cover, every filtered photo plants a "55" that says, this is what beautiful looks like. This is what desirable looks like. You don't measure up. Women are taught to commodify themselves, to present their bodies as products, to compete in a marketplace where youth and beauty are currency and aging is bankruptcy.

The erosion of consent is subtle but devastating. The "55s" normalize coercion. They romanticize persistence. They teach women that saying "no" makes them prudish, that having boundaries makes them difficult, and that withholding sex makes them manipulative. The message is clear: Your body is not fully yours. Access to you is expected. Resistance is unreasonable.

And so women enter relationships confused about their own worth, uncertain about their own boundaries, and conditioned to perform desirability rather than steward intimacy. They give their bodies while guarding their hearts, not realizing that God designed the two to move together.

The gendered "55s" create a tragic collision: men conditioned to consume, meeting women conditioned to be consumed. Both are victims of the same con, but neither recognizes the con artist's hand.

The Spiritual Consequence: Why This Isn't Just Psychology.

Here's what the world won't tell you: you are not a body with a spirit. You are a spirit with a body.

This distinction matters. If you're just a body with a spirit, then sexual sin is merely a psychological issue, a matter of self-control, willpower, or therapy. But if you're a spirit with a body, then sexual sin is a spiritual issue, a matter of covenant, authority, and eternal consequence.

The "55s" planted by culture don't just affect your mind; they affect your spirit. Every sexual image you consume, every lustful thought you entertain, every boundary you compromise, these aren't just psychological events. They are spiritual transactions. You are not just forming habits; you are forming agreements. You are not just making choices; you are opening doors.

Scripture is clear: "Flee fornication. Every sin that a man doeth is without the body; but he that committeth fornication sinneth against his own body" (1 Corinthians 6:18). Why is sexual sin different? Because it's not just an external act, it's an internal violation. It's a sin against the temple. It's a defilement of the dwelling place of the Holy Spirit.

The hyper-sexual delusion isn't just teaching you the wrong facts about sex; it's teaching you the wrong theology about yourself. It tells you that your body is yours to do with as you please, that pleasure is the highest good, that intimacy is a recreational activity rather than a sacred covenant. This is spiritual miseducation at its finest.

And the enemy knows exactly what he's doing. He doesn't need to drag you into obvious, blatant rebellion. He just needs to plant enough "55s" that you walk into defilement thinking it's freedom. He just needs to normalize enough compromise that you cross covenant lines without even realizing you've moved.

The "55s" aren't just shaping your behavior; they're shaping your spiritual agreements. They're determining what you give access to, what you come into covenant with, and what you allow to attach to your bloodline. And most people don't even realize the transaction has occurred until they're already bound.

You've Been Conned, But You're Not Alone

If you're reading this and recognizing yourself in these words, take a breath. You're not crazy. You're not weak. You're not uniquely broken.

You've been conned.

And the con was sophisticated. It didn't announce itself. It didn't ask permission. It didn't give you a chance to opt out. It started before you were old enough to recognize it, and it's been running in the background of your life ever since.

Maybe you've felt the weight of shame, knowing that your thought life doesn't match your confession, that your private struggles contradict your public testimony. Maybe you've tried to "do better," to "stop," to "get free," only to find yourself back in the same cycle weeks or months later. Maybe you've wondered if you're too far gone, if you've crossed too many lines, if God could ever really use someone with your history.

Here's the truth: the shame you feel is real, but it's not the final word. The conviction you sense is the Holy Spirit, not condemnation. The struggle you're in is evidence that you're still alive spiritually, that you haven't fully surrendered to the delusion, that there's a part of you that still recognizes the con.

You didn't choose to be targeted. You didn't ask for the "55s" to be planted. You didn't design the culture you were born into. But you are responsible for what you do next.

The good news is this: once you see the con, you can't unsee it. Once you recognize the "55s," you can start dismantling them. Once you understand the mechanics of how you were deceived, you can begin the process of walking out of deception and into truth.

This book isn't about condemnation. It's about liberation. It's about exposing the con so thoroughly that you can finally make free choices, real choices, not reactions to planted suggestions. It's about reclaiming your sexuality from the enemy's distortion and restoring it to God's original design.

But before we can talk about restoration, we need to talk about foundation. Before we can rebuild, we need to understand what we're made of. Before we can walk in sexual wholeness, we need to understand the mechanics of the soul.

The Path Forward: Understanding Your Design

The world has spent your entire life telling you what sex is. It's time to hear from the One who created it. To dismantle the hyper-sexual delusion, you must first understand how you were made. You must understand the distinction between your physical element and your spiritual essence. You must grasp the mechanics of covenant, the power of blood, and the reality of spiritual portals.

This isn't abstract theology. This is the blueprint of your design. And once you see it, everything changes. In the next chapter, we'll explore the two Hebrew concepts that define your existence: Asa and Bara. We'll unpack what it means to be fashioned from dust and filled with the breath of God. We'll examine why sexual intimacy isn't just a physical act but a spiritual fusion. And we'll begin to see why the enemy has worked so hard to distort your understanding of sex, because he knows that if you ever grasp the true power of covenant intimacy, you become unstoppable.

The con is over. The truth is coming.

Let's begin…

Chapter 2

The Mechanics of the Soul:

Asa and Bara

Understanding the Physical and Spiritual Mechanics of Human Creation

Chapter 2: The Mechanics of the Soul: Asa and Bara

To understand why this cultural "con" is so dangerous, we must look at how God built us. Theological scholarship often fails to distinguish between the two Hebrew concepts of our creation: Asa and Bara.

Asa: This refers to your physical element, the part of you fashioned from the dust of the earth.

Bara: This is the divine aspect; the very spirit of God breathed into your humanity.

When you engage in sexual intimacy, you aren't just performing a physical act; you are uniting your Bara and your Asa with another person. You are fusing your spiritual essence with theirs. This is why the Bible warns that he who is joined to a harlot becomes "one body". This isn't a metaphor; it is a spiritual mechanic.

The Portal of the Blood Covenant

Sex is, in its purest form, a blood covenant, the strongest type of agreement in existence. It is a divine agreement rooted in purpose, not just pleasure. When you enter this covenant outside of God's design, you aren't just connecting with a person; you are opening a spiritual portal to everything in that person's history.

If you unite with someone who carries a history of trauma, addiction, or generational iniquity, you are essentially saying, "Lord, whatever is in them, I want it in me". You become a part of a "deep and intricate web" of past partners and old covenants that continue to affect your fears, fantasies, and expectations today.

The Pathway to Newness

The good news of the charismatic faith is that no covenant is too old for the blood of Jesus to break. If you find yourself "tethered to old covenants" even within a current marriage, there is a way out. The Bible declares that in Christ, you are a new creation; the old things have passed away.

Your journey to sexual wholeness begins by acknowledging these "unspoken oaths" and preparing to "leave" the ideologies of the world so you can truly "cleave" to the life God intended for you.

Why the World Wants You to Forget Your Bara

The culture has spent billions of dollars convincing you that you are only Asa, only body, only flesh, only physical matter responding to physical stimuli. This is not an accident. This is a strategy.

If the enemy can get you to believe that sex is merely a physical act, friction, chemistry, dopamine, oxytocin, then he can get you to treat it like any other physical appetite. Hungry? Eat. Thirsty? Drink. Aroused? Have sex. It's just biology. It's just natural. It's just your body doing what it does.

But you are not just a body.

You are Bara, divine breath, eternal spirit, the image of God housed in flesh. Your body is the instrument, but your spirit is the musician. And when you reduce yourself to only Asa, you're like a concert hall that only acknowledges the speakers but denies the existence of the sound waves. You see the equipment, but you miss the music. You feel the vibration, but you can't explain the resonance.

This is why the "55s" from Chapter 1 work so effectively. They train you to see sex as performance, as conquest, as transaction, as entertainment, all Asa categories. They never mention Bara because acknowledging Bara would expose the con. If you realized that every sexual encounter is a spiritual event, you would approach intimacy with the reverence it deserves. You would recognize that you're not just sharing your body, you're sharing your eternity.

The tragedy of our generation is not that people are having sex. The tragedy is that people are having sex while believing they are only having sex. They think they're engaging in a recreational activity when in reality they're performing a sacred ritual. They think they're making a casual choice when, in fact, they're entering a binding covenant.

Scripture is clear: "Know ye not that your body is the temple of the Holy Ghost, which is in you, which ye have of God, and ye are not your own?" (1 Corinthians 6:19). Your body is not a playground. It's a sanctuary. And every person you allow into that sanctuary doesn't just touch your flesh; they touch your altar.

The world wants you spiritually blind to your Bara nature because spiritual blindness makes you vulnerable. If you can't see the spiritual dimension of sex, you can't protect yourself from spiritual consequences. You'll walk into covenant agreements thinking you're just "having fun." You'll open portals thinking you're just "exploring your sexuality." You'll bind yourself to bloodlines, thinking you're just "living your truth."

And by the time you realize what you've done, the damage is already generational.

The Mechanics of Blood Covenant: Why Sex Is Never "Just Sex"

In the ancient world, a blood covenant was the most sacred,

binding agreement two parties could enter. It wasn't a contract you could break without a penalty. It wasn't a handshake you could walk away from. It was a fusion of identities, a merging of destinies, a declaration that said, "What's mine is yours, and what's yours is mine, forever."

When Abraham entered into a covenant with God, blood was shed (Genesis 15). When David and Jonathan entered into a covenant, they exchanged weapons and garments and made a blood oath (1 Samuel 18). The blood covenant wasn't symbolic. It was a mechanic. It created a legal, spiritual bond that transcended emotion, circumstance, and even death.

Sex is a blood covenant.

Not metaphorically. Not poetically. Literally. The breaking of the hymen, the exchange of fluids, the mingling of DNA, these are not incidental details. They are covenant markers. They are the physical evidence of a spiritual transaction. When two people have sex, they are not just experiencing pleasure. They are entering into a physical and spiritual agreement. They are saying, with their bodies, "I am yours, and you are mine."

The problem Is that most people enter this covenant without understanding what they're agreeing to. Marriage is a blood covenant sealed by God. It is witnessed, blessed, and sanctioned by divine authority. The covenant is not just between two people: it's between two people and God. This is why Jesus said, "What therefore God hath joined together, let not man put asunder" (Matthew 19:6). The covenant is unbreakable because God Himself is the guarantor.

But sex outside of marriage is a blood covenant sealed by self. It still creates a bond. It still opens a portal. It still merges identities. But it does so without divine covering, without spiritual protection, without the boundaries that sustain a covenant. You get all the binding with none of the blessing. You get all the fusion without any foundation.

This is why Paul warns, "Know ye not that he which is joined to a harlot is one body? for two, saith he, shall be one flesh" (1 Corinthians 6:16). Notice he doesn't say, "He who marries a harlot." He says, "He who is joined to a harlot." The act itself creates the bond. The covenant is activated the moment the blood is exchanged, whether you intended it or not, whether you acknowledged it or not, whether you even believed in it or not.

Sex always creates a covenant. The only question is whether that covenant is sanctioned by God or hijacked by the enemy.

When you have sex, you are making hidden agreements. You

are consenting to more than physical intimacy. You are consenting to spiritual and physical entanglement having effects in the soul. You are saying, "Whatever is in you, I receive. Whatever is in your bloodline, I welcome. Whatever assignments are on your life, I participate in them." Most people would never consciously agree to these terms. But they agree to them every time they have sex outside of covenant.

The Portal Metaphor: What You're Actually Opening

A portal is not a feeling. It's not a vibe. It's not an emotional connection.

A portal is a legal opening, a spiritual doorway that grants access between two realms. In the natural world, we understand this concept easily. The door in your house is a portal. It allows passage from outside to inside. If you leave that door open, anything can walk through, invited or not.

Sex opens a portal between your spirit and another person's spirit. And once that portal is open, it doesn't automatically close when the act is over. It remains open until it is intentionally closed through repentance, renunciation, and the blood of Jesus.

This is why you can't just "move on" from a sexual relationship. This is why people talk about their exes years later with the same emotional intensity as if the breakup happened yesterday. This is why you can be in a new relationship but still feel spiritually tethered to an old one. The portal is still open. The covenant is still active. The access is still granted.

And here's what makes this even more complex: when you open a portal to another person, you're not just opening a portal to them. You're opening a portal to their entire lineage, their parents, their grandparents, their great-grandparents, and every unhealed wound, every generational habit, every spiritual assignment that has been passed down through their bloodline. You think you're just sleeping with one person. But spiritually, you're merging with a family tree.

This is why some people report inheriting depression after a sexual encounter with someone who struggled with mental illness. This is why addiction patterns can transfer from one partner to another. This is why trauma responses; fear, anxiety, rage, can suddenly manifest in someone who never experienced the original trauma. The portal doesn't just connect you to the person. It connects you to their history.

And shame compounds the problem. Shame keeps the portal

open longer because shame prevents you from addressing the covenant. You can't break what you won't acknowledge. You can't close what you're too ashamed to admit is open. So, the portal remains active, the access remains granted, and the entanglement deepens with every passing year.

In the spiritual realm, covenants create legal rights. When you enter a blood covenant with someone, you are granting them legal access to your life. And if that person has granted access to demonic assignments, addictions, or generational iniquity, those things now have legal access to you. Not because you're weak. Not because you're cursed. But because you opened the door.

The good news is that legal rights can be revoked. Portals can be closed. Covenants can be broken. But first, you have to understand the mechanics of what you're dealing with.

One Flesh, Multiple Histories: The Cumulative Entanglement

When Scripture says that two become "one flesh," it's not describing a romantic ideal. It's describing a spiritual mechanic. One flesh means fusion. It means that your identity and their identity are no longer separate. It means that what affects them affects you. It means that their history becomes your history, their struggles become your struggles, and their spiritual assignments become your spiritual assignments.

This is beautiful within the context of covenant marriage. It's the foundation of partnership, intimacy, and generational legacy. But outside of covenant, it's devastating. Because you're not just merging with one person. You're merging with everyone they've ever merged with.

If your partner has had five previous sexual partners, you are not entering a relationship with one person. You are entering a relationship with six bloodlines. You are inheriting the spiritual residue of every covenant they've ever made, every portal they've ever opened, every agreement they've ever entered, whether they remember it or not, whether they regret it or not, whether they've "moved on" or not.

This is why some relationships feel spiritually heavy even when they're emotionally satisfying. You can love someone deeply and still feel weighed down by their presence. You can be attracted to someone physically and still feel drained by their energy. It's not that they're bad people. It's that their unhealed history is now entangled with your present.

The cumulative effect is staggering. If you've had multiple partners, and each of those partners had multiple partners, you are carrying the spiritual residue of dozens, potentially hundreds, of bloodlines. You are walking around with a web of covenants you never consciously agreed to, portals you never intentionally opened, and legal rights you never knowingly granted.

And the enemy is using every single one of them to keep you bound.

Why This Matters for Your Healing Journey

If you've made it this far and you're feeling overwhelmed, take a breath. This is not condemnation. This is revelation.

Understanding the mechanics of Asa and Bara, blood covenant, and spiritual portals is not meant to shame you. It's meant to empower you. Once you understand how the system works, you can begin dismantling it.

You are not broken. You are entangled.

You are not hopelessly sinful. You are spiritually bound.

You are not too far gone. You are standing at the threshold of freedom.

This reframe changes everything. Shame tells you that you're defective, that something is fundamentally wrong with you, that you'll never be free. But truth tells you that you're dealing with a mechanic, and mechanics can be reversed.

You didn't know what you were doing when you opened those portals. You didn't understand the covenant you were entering. You didn't realize the legal rights you were granting.

But now you do. And knowledge is the first step toward freedom.

The reason most people stay stuck in sexual bondage is not because they lack willpower. It's because they're trying to fight a spiritual battle with emotional weapons. They're trying to close portals they don't even know are open. They're trying to break covenants they've never acknowledged. But you can't close what you can't see. And you can't break what you won't name.

This chapter has given you the language to see and the framework to name. You now understand that sex is not just a physical act; it's a spiritual transaction. You now understand that every sexual encounter creates a covenant, opens a portal, and grants legal access. You now understand that you're not just dealing with your own history, you're dealing with the cumulative history of everyone you've ever been intimate with.

And here's the hope: there is a way to close the portals. There is a way to break the covenants. There is a way to revoke the legal rights and walk into the freedom that Jesus purchased for you.

But before we can talk about how to close the portals, we need to talk about where the portals are. We need to identify the specific covenants that are keeping you bound. We need to diagnose the entanglements, so we know exactly what we're breaking. And that's where the Woman at the Well comes in.

In the next chapter, we'll explore the most profound diagnostic moment in Scripture, the moment when Jesus looked at a woman with five failed relationships and one current entanglement and said, "Go, call your husband." We'll unpack the strategy He used to expose her covenants, identify her portals, and set her on the path to freedom.

Because once you see the pattern, you can break the cycle. Once you identify the portals, you can close them. Once you understand the covenants, you can renounce them.

The mechanics are clear. The diagnosis is next.
Let's continue.

Chapter 3

The Mastery of The Blood Covenant

Why Sex is the ultimate spiritual agreement and how it creates a fusion of destinies.

Chapter 3: The Diagnostic Moment

You now understand the mechanics. You know about Asa and Bara. You know that sex creates blood covenant. You know that every sexual union opens a portal, not just to a person, but to their entire bloodline. You know that these portals don't close automatically, that they remain spiritually active even after the relationship ends. You know that the cumulative effect of multiple covenants creates spiritual entanglement so complex that most people can't even identify where their own thoughts end and someone else's begin.

The mechanics are clear. Now comes the harder part: the diagnosis. Because understanding how the system works is not the same as recognizing where you are in the system. And most believers, even those who intellectually agree with everything we've covered so far, are still in denial about the specific covenants they're carrying. They'll nod along when we talk about "the culture" or "other people's mistakes," but when it comes to naming their own Five, the room goes silent. This chapter is that silence broken.

The Woman at the Well is not an ancient cautionary tale. She is a mirror. Her story is not unique; it's universal. The details change, but the pattern remains the same. Five failed covenants. One current entanglement. And a soul so exhausted from carrying the weight of unhealed history that she can't even draw water at the normal time of day.

Men carry this pattern. Women carry this pattern. Married people carry this pattern. Singles carry this pattern. The person sitting in the pew next to you on Sunday morning is likely carrying this pattern. And if you've had more than one sexual partner in your life, whether through fornication, adultery, or even remarriage after divorce, you are carrying some version of this pattern too.

The number isn't always five. Sometimes it's three. Sometimes it's ten. But the structure is almost always the same: a series of relationships that follow a predictable spiritual sequence, each one compounding the damage of the one before, each one widening the portal, each one adding another layer of entanglement that makes true intimacy feel impossible.

This is not about shame. This is about recognition. You cannot heal what you will not acknowledge. You cannot break what you will not name. And the enemy's greatest weapon is not the covenants themselves; it's your refusal to admit they're still active.

So, let's do what Jesus did at the well. Let's bring the Five into the light. Let's identify the pattern. Let's name the covenants.

Not to condemn you, but to free you. Because the Woman at the Well didn't leave that conversation in shame, she left it in power. Her wound became her witness. Her past became her platform. And the same can be true for you.

But first, you have to be willing to say it out loud: "I have had five husbands. And the one I have now is not my husband."

The Seventh Man is waiting. But He won't force His way in. He's waiting for you to open the door.

The Spiritual Weight of the Five

The Woman at the Well didn't just have five failed relationships. She was carrying five open covenants, five spiritual tethers that bound her to men who were no longer physically present but remained spiritually active in her life. Each union had left a mark, not just on her emotions, but on her soul. And the cumulative weight of those marks was crushing her.

The First was the one who opened the portal. For many, this is the relationship marked by trauma, premature exposure, or the shattering of innocence. The First creates the template, the spiritual frequency, that all future relationships will echo. If the First was violent, future partners may carry violence. If the First was abandoned, future partners will trigger abandonment. The First doesn't just take your virginity; he takes your baseline. He sets the frequency your soul will resonate with until that frequency is intentionally broken.

The Rebound was the one she ran to in order to numb the pain of the First. This is the relationship built on desperation, not desire. The Rebound is never about the person; it's about the escape. But instead of healing, the Rebound compounds the wound. Now she's not just carrying the trauma of the First; she's carrying the shame of using someone else to medicate it. The Rebound adds guilt to the grief, and the portal widens.

The Mirror, *the third man*, was the one who reflected her own brokenness back at her. This is the relationship in which she saw herself clearly for the first time and hated what she saw. The Mirror didn't cause her insecurity; he revealed it. He was emotionally unavailable because she was emotionally unavailable. He was afraid of commitment because she feared being known. The Mirror showed her that she wasn't just a victim of bad men; she was participating in a pattern. And that realization was unbearable.

The Habit was the two men who became a ritual rather than a relationship. This is the partner who stayed too long, not because of love, but because of familiarity. The Habit is the relationship you keep returning to even when you know it's dead. It's the ex you text at 2 a.m. It's the person you can't quite let go of because letting go would mean admitting you wasted years. The Habit isn't passionate, it's pathological. And it trains your soul to confuse comfort with covenant.

The Current is the one who "is not your husband" the person she's with now, the one paying the price for the ghosts of the previous five. The Current is often a good person trapped in a bad system. He doesn't understand why she flinches when he touches her. He doesn't know why intimacy feels heavy instead of freeing. He doesn't realize that when he looks into her eyes, he's staring at a room full of men he's never met. The Current is being punished for crimes he didn't commit, and the relationship is suffocating under the weight of unhealed history.

By the time the Woman at the Well encountered Jesus, she wasn't just tired. She was spiritually exhausted. She had given pieces of herself to five different men, and each piece had taken a part of her she couldn't get back. She was fragmented, hollowed out, a shell of the woman God designed her to be. And the shame was so thick she couldn't even draw water at the normal time of day.

She came to the well at noon, the hottest, most uncomfortable hour, because she couldn't bear to face the other women. She knew what they whispered. She knew the looks they gave.

She had become the cautionary tale, the woman whose name was synonymous with scandal. And in her isolation, the enemy convinced her that this was all she would ever be.

This is the spiritual weight of the Five. It's not just regret. It's not just heartbreak. It's the suffocating reality of carrying multiple open covenants, multiple unhealed wounds, multiple frequencies all playing at once in your soul. It's the exhaustion of pretending you're fine when you're barely holding yourself together. It's the loneliness of being surrounded by people but feeling utterly unknown. And it's the trap that millions of believers are living in right now.

Why the "One" Cannot Fix the "Five"

The most dangerous lie the enemy tells broken people is this: The right person will heal your past. The Woman at the Well believed this lie. That's why she kept trying. That's why, after five failed marriages, she was still in a relationship. She thought, maybe this one will be different. Maybe this one will finally fill the void. Maybe this one will make me forget the others.

But “One" cannot fix the "Five." And the reason is simple: you cannot build a healthy covenant on top of unhealed covenants. You cannot plant a garden in soil that's still full of roots from dead trees. You cannot expect a new relationship to thrive when the old relationships are still spiritually active.

This is the Cumulative Covenant Effect in action. Every sexual union you've ever had is still present in your soul until it is intentionally severed. The people may be gone, but the covenants remain. The relationships may have ended, but the portals are still open. And when you bring those open portals into a new relationship, you're not giving your partner access to you; you're giving them access to everyone you've ever been with.

The Current always pays the price for the Five. He walks into what he thinks is a relationship with one person, only to discover he's in a relationship with a crowd. He tries to love her, but she can't receive it because her soul is still tethered to the men who hurt her. He tries to be intimate with her, but the bedroom feels haunted. He tries to build a future with her, but she keeps sabotaging it because deep down, she doesn't believe she deserves to be loved.

And the tragic irony is that the Current often becomes the Sixth, another failed relationship, another open portal, another layer of shame added to the pile.

This is why "true love" doesn't erase spiritual entanglement. Love is powerful, but it's not a substitute for deliverance. You can marry the godliest, patient, compassionate person in the world, and if you haven't closed the portals from your past, that marriage will still feel heavy. The intimacy will still feel forced. The connection will still feel fractured. Because you're not just dealing with emotional baggage, you're dealing with spiritual bondage.

The marriage bed is supposed to be "undefiled" (Hebrews 13:4), but how can it be undefiled when you're bringing defiled covenants into it? How can it be a place of rest when it's crowded with the ghosts of past lovers? How can it be a sanctuary when the portals are still open?

The answer is: it can't. Not until the Five are identified, renounced, and severed. This is why so many marriages that look good on paper feel broken in practice. This is why so many couples who "did everything right", courted, prayed, waited, still struggle with intimacy. It's not that they don't love each other. It's that one or both of them are still carrying unhealed covenants, and those covenants are poisoning the present.

The "One" cannot fix the "Five" because the "One" is human. And humans, no matter how loving, no matter how patient, cannot break spiritual covenants. Only Jesus can do that. Only the Seventh Man can set you free.

The Seventh Man and the Frequency of Freedom

When the Woman at the Well met Jesus, she didn't know she was meeting the Seventh Man. She thought He was just another traveler, another man who would want something from her. But Jesus was different. He didn't want her body. He wanted her freedom.

In biblical numerology, seven is the number of completion, perfection, and rest. It's the number of the Sabbath; the day God rested after creation. It's the number of covenant fulfillments, the number that signals the end of a cycle and the beginning of something new. The Woman at the Well had been trapped in a cycle of five failed marriages and one broken relationship, six incomplete unions. But when she encountered Jesus, the Seventh Man, the cycle was broken.

The Seventh Man offers what the first six could not: wholeness without possession. The First took her innocence. The Rebound took her dignity. The Mirror took her hope. The Habits took her years. The Current took her peace. But the Seventh Man? He gave. He gave her living water. He gave her truth. He gave her a future. And He asked for nothing in return except that she receive it. This is the radical difference between Jesus and every other relationship you've ever had. Every other relationship has been transactional. Every other person has wanted something from you; your body, your time, your energy, your validation. But Jesus doesn't need anything from you. He's complete in Himself. He doesn't come to take; He comes to restore.

And here's the most powerful part of the story: Jesus knew everything about her. He knew about the five husbands. He knew about the Current. He knew about the shame, the secrets, the scandals. He knew it all, and He still chose her. "You have well said, 'I have no husband,' for you have had five husbands, and the one whom you now have is not your husband; in that you spoke truly" (John 4:17-18).

This wasn't condemnation. This was recognition. Jesus wasn't exposing her to shame her. He was exposing her to free her. Because you cannot heal what you will not acknowledge. You cannot break what you will not name. And the Woman at the Well had spent years hiding, pretending, covering up the truth. But in the presence of the Seventh Man, the truth became the pathway to freedom.

She didn't have to perform for Him. She didn't have to pretend to be someone she wasn't. She didn't have to hide her past or minimize her pain. He saw all of it, and He loved her anyway. Not because of what she could give Him, but because of who He was.

This is the frequency of freedom. It's the frequency of being fully known and fully loved. It's the frequency of rest, of Sabbath, of completion. And when you encounter the Seventh Man, when you stop trying to fix yourself with another relationship and instead surrender to the One who can actually heal you, everything changes.

The Seventh Man doesn't just forgive your past. He redeems it. He doesn't just close the portals. He fills them with His presence. He doesn't just break the covenants. He replaces them with a new covenant, one that cannot be broken, one that cannot fail, one that will never leave you empty.

The Pathway to Healing

Healing from the Cumulative Covenant Effect requires three intentional steps: Identification, Renunciation, and Invocation. Identification is the act of naming the Five. You cannot cast out what you will not name. You cannot break what you will not acknowledge. You cannot bind what you do not see. This is why Jesus asked the woman, "Go, call your husband" (John 4:16). He wasn't cruel. He was forcing her to confront what was real. He was making her identify the covenants that were keeping her bound.

You must do the same. You must name the relationships. You must acknowledge the portals. You must identify the covenants, not to wallow in shame, but to sever them. Write them down if you have to. Speak to them out loud. Bring them to the light. Because what remains hidden remains active.

Renunciation is the act of breaking agreement with the Five. This is where you declare, "I renounce the covenant I made with [name of your five]. I break agreement with every word spoken, every vow made, every portal opened. I revoke the legal rights I granted, and I close the door in Jesus' name." This isn't a formula. This is a legal declaration in the spiritual realm. You are revoking access. You are closing portals. You are severing ties.

Invocation is the act of calling on the Seventh Man. This is where you invite Jesus into the places that were once occupied by others. You ask Him to fill the voids, heal the wounds, and restore what was stolen. You declare, "Jesus, you are my completion. You are my Sabbath rest. You are the One who makes me whole." And you receive the living water He offers, not as a transaction, but as a gift.

The Woman at the Well didn't just receive healing that day. She received a new identity. She went from being the woman with five husbands to being the woman who encountered the Messiah. She went from hiding in shame to running into the city with a testimony. She went from being defined by her past to being empowered by her future.

And here's the most beautiful part: her five husbands became her witness-bearers. The very thing that had been her greatest source of shame became her greatest platform for ministry. "Come, see a Man who told me all things that I ever did. Could this be the Christ?" (John 4:29). The whole city came to Jesus because of her testimony. Her wound became her witness. Her brokenness became her breakthrough.

This is what happens when you encounter the Seventh Man. Your past doesn't disqualify you, it positions you. Your pain doesn't define you, it refines you. Your shame doesn't silence you, it becomes your story.

The pathway to healing is not complicated. It's not a 12-step program or a years-long therapy process. It's a divine encounter with the One who knows everything about you and loves you anyway. It's the moment you stop running, stop hiding, stop pretending, and you let Him see you. All of you. The Five. The Current. The shame. The secrets. All of it. And when He sees you, He doesn't condemn you. He says, "I know. And I'm here to set you free." The healing has already begun. The Seventh Man is already here. The only question is: will you let Him in?

The Generational Portal

Understanding the Mechanics of Iniquity

In the Charismatic tradition, we understand that we are not just individuals; we are the sum of a lineage. We carry the DNA of our ancestors, but we also carry their spiritual momentum. While we celebrate the "blessings of Abraham," we must also contend with the "iniquities of the fathers." The Bible is clear: “For I, the Lord your God, am a jealous God, visiting the iniquity of the fathers upon the children to the third and fourth generations of those who hate Me” (Exodus 20:5).

The Portal vs. The Sin

Most people view sexual sin as a momentary lapse in judgment. But in the realm of the Spirit, sex is a portal. Think of a portal as a legal doorway. When you engage in a sexual union outside of the covenant of marriage, you aren't just "having an experience." You are opening a door in your soul. If the person you are joining with has an open door to a generational spirit, whether it be a spirit of rejection, addiction, or perversion, that spirit now has a "legal right" to walk through the portal and enter your life.

This is why you may find yourself struggling with a specific fantasy or a heavy depression that "isn't yours." You didn't create it; you inherited it through a portal.

The Bloodline and the Bed

Your "Bloodline" is the highway of your heritage. Sexual intimacy is the "merging of highways." When two people become "one flesh," their bloodlines intersect.

The Asa (Physical) Intersection: You share DNA and physical health.

The Bara (Spiritual) Intersection: You share spiritual history and "altars."

If your partner's lineage has a "ritual" of divorce or a history of secret abuse, that "frequency" begins to vibrate in your own life. You may notice that after a specific relationship, your prayer life feels "clogged" or your sense of divine purpose feels "veiled." This is the Portal Effect. You have allowed a generational "pollutant" into your stream.

Closing the Portal

The beauty of the Gospel is that while the "first Adam" opened portals of death, the "Last Adam" (Jesus) provides a Blood that cleanses the portal entirely.

To heal, we must do more than just "stop the act." We must:

Identify the Entry Point: When did this "weight" first enter your life?

Repent for the Lineage: Standing in the gap for the sins of the portal-openers.

Sever the Soul Tie: Using the authority of the Believer to "uncouple" your Bara from the iniquity of the partner.

Healing is not just about being "good" it's about being clean. It's about ensuring that when you finally "cleave" to your spouse, you are bringing a pure portal to the marriage bed.

PART II: THE DIAGNOSIS OF THE SOUL

Chapter 4: The Woman at the Well Strategy

Identifying the 'Five Husbands' and the cumulative weight of past covenants

Chapter 4: The Art of Leaving

Severing the Ties that Bind the Soul

The scripture gives us a blueprint for covenant intimacy that most people skip over in their rush to get to the good part: "For this cause shall a man leave father and mother and shall cleave to his wife: and they twain shall be one flesh" (Matthew 19:5). We love the "one flesh" part. We preach it at weddings. We quote it in marriage counseling. We use it to justify why sex matters. But we conveniently ignore the first instruction: leave.

Not "leave eventually." Not "leave when it feels right." Not "leave after you've tried everything else." Leave first. Before the cleaving. Before the covenant. Before the one flesh union that everyone is so eager to experience. Because here's the truth most people don't want to hear: you cannot cleave to something new while you're still tethered to something old. You cannot build a holy altar on ground that's already occupied. You cannot invite the presence of God into a space that's still hosting the ghosts of your past.

The order matters. Leaving precedes cleaving. Always. And if you try to skip this step, if you try to cleave while you're still spiritually, emotionally, and generationally bound to the Five, you don't create intimacy. You create a tug-of-war. A spiritual tension so severe that it eventually tears the soul apart.

This is why so many marriages feel like battlegrounds. This is why so many believers struggle with intimacy even after they've "done everything right." This is why the Woman at the Well couldn't receive living water until she acknowledged the Five. Because you cannot drink from a new well while you're still carrying water from the old ones. Leaving is not optional. It is the foundation. And until you master the art of leaving, you will never experience the power of cleaving.

The Cultural Parents You Must Divorce

When the Bible says to leave "father and mother," it's not just talking about your biological parents. It's talking about the ideologies, patterns, and spiritual authorities that birthed your current identity. It's talking about the voices that shaped your understanding of sex, intimacy, shame, and worth long before you ever opened this book.

In your journey toward sexual healing, your "Cultural Parents" are not people. They are systems. And they have been raising you, feeding you, disciplining you, defining you, since you were old enough to absorb a message. Let me introduce you to the three most common Cultural Parents that must be divorced before true healing can begin.

The Mother of Shame

She is the voice that whispers in the dark. The one that tells you your body is inherently dirty. That your past makes you unlovable. That you are "damaged goods" and no amount of repentance will ever make you clean enough for God to fully use you.

The Mother of Shame doesn't sound like condemnation. She sounds like concern. She sounds like wisdom. She sounds like she's protecting you from further harm by reminding you of every mistake you've ever made.

She shows up in the mirror when you're getting dressed. She shows up in the bedroom when your spouse reaches for you. She shows up in church when the worship gets too intimate, and you feel like a fraud for lifting your hands. She shows up every single time you try to step into freedom, and she reminds you: "You don't deserve this. You know what you did. You know who you were."

The Mother of Shame is not your biological mother, though she may have used your mother's voice to gain access. She is a generational spirit. A principality. A stronghold that has been operating in your bloodline for decades, maybe centuries. And she will not leave voluntarily.

You must divorce her. You must revoke her authority legally

and spiritually. You must stand in the gap and declare: "You no longer have jurisdiction over my body, my bed, or my future. I am not who I was. I am who God says I am. And you are evicted."

The Father of Lust

He is louder than the mother of Shame, but just as insidious. He is the voice that tells you that your worth is tied to your desirability. That intimacy is performance. That sex is conquest. That your body is a tool for validation, and if you're not using it, you're wasting it.

The Father of Lust is the one who planted the "55s" we talked about in Chapter 1. He is the architect of the hyper-sexual delusion. He is the one who taught you that love is measured in intensity, that passion is the same as connection, and that if it doesn't feel like a movie scene, it's not real.

He shows up in your thought life. In your fantasies. In the way you scroll through social media comparing your relationship to everyone else's highlight reel. He shows up in the way you dress, the way you flirt, the way you measure your worth by how many people want you.

And here's the trap: the Father of Lust doesn't feel like sin. He feels like he is free. He feels empowered. He feels like you're finally taking control of your sexuality instead of letting religion shame you into submission.

But freedom that requires constant validation is not freedom; it's addiction. And empowerment that depends on someone else's desire is not power, it's slavery.

The Father of Lust must be divorced. Not because desire is bad. Not because sexuality is evil. But because he has twisted the gift into a weapon, and until you sever that covenant, you will never experience sex the way God designed it: as worship, not warfare.

The Ancestral Altar

This is the hardest one to identify because it doesn't have a voice. It has a pattern. It's the generational portal we explored in Chapter 3; the one that demands you repeat the mistakes of your lineage even when you consciously know better.

The Ancestral Altar is why your grandmother's failed marriage looks eerily similar to your mother's failed marriage, which looks eerily similar to your own. It's why you keep choosing the same type of partner even though you swore you'd never do it again. It's why you can quote scripture about purity but still find yourself in the same compromising situations your father was in thirty years ago.

The Ancestral Altar doesn't care about your intentions. It cares about your bloodline. And as long as that altar remains active, as long as those covenants remain unbroken, you are not just fighting your own flesh, you are fighting the accumulated spiritual debt of everyone who came before you.

This is why some people can go to therapy for years, read every book, attend every conference, and still feel stuck. Because they're trying to heal a personal wound when the real issue is a generational habit. They're trying to close a door when the entire foundation is built on an open portal.

The Ancestral Altar must be dismantled. Not honored. Not managed. Dismantled. You must stand in the gap, repent for the sins of your fathers, and break the covenant that gave that altar legal rights to your life.

The Wilderness of the Soul

Here's what no one tells you about leaving: it's terrifying.

Not because you love the thing you're leaving. But because you've grown accustomed to it. You know its rhythm. You know its voice. You know how to navigate its dysfunction. And even though it's killing you, at least it's familiar.

When you leave, when you truly sever the ties to the Cultural Parents, when you close the portals, when you renounce the covenants, you enter what I call the Wilderness of the Soul. You have left Egypt, but you haven't reached the Promised Land. You are in the in-between. The liminal space. The place where the old is gone, but the new hasn't fully manifested yet. And it is silent.

Devastatingly, unbearably silent.

The voices that used to fill your head, the shame, the lust, the generational whispers, are gone. But so is the noise. So is the distraction. So is the false sense of identity that those voices provided. And in that silence, you are forced to confront the question you've been avoiding your entire life: Who am I without dysfunction?

This is why so many people return to unholy sexual cycles. Not because they want the sin. But because they cannot tolerate the silence. They cannot sit in the emptiness long enough for God to fill it. They panic. They assume the silence means they've done something wrong, that God has abandoned them, that healing isn't real.

So, they go back. They reopen the portal. They re-invite the Cultural Parents. They pick up the waterpot they left at the well and carry it back to the same broken cistern, because at least the weight is familiar.

But here's the truth: the silence is not abandoned. The silence is preparation. God is clearing the land. He is demolishing the old structures so He can build something new. And if you fill that space prematurely, if you rush to fill the void with another relationship, another distraction, another coping mechanism, you will abort the very thing God is trying to birth in you. The Wilderness is not punishment. It is purification. And the only way through it is to sit in the silence long enough to hear the voice of the Seventh Man calling you forward.

The Spiritual Bill of Divorcement

Moses allowed a "writing of divorce" because of the hardness of hearts (Matthew 19:8). Jesus pointed us back to the original design; no divorce, one flesh, covenant for life. But there is a powerful spiritual principle hidden in that allowance, one that applies directly to your healing journey:

You must sign a spiritual divorce from your past.

Not from the people. From the agreements. From the identities. From the covenants that were never meant to be made in the first place. This is the act of leaving. It is not passive. It is not gradual. It is a conscious, prophetic declaration where you legally and spiritually sever the ties that have been binding on your soul. And it happens in three steps:

Renounce the Agreement

You must name the lie you've been living under and revoke your consent. This is not the same as repentance. Repentance is turning away from sin. Renunciation is canceling the contract.

"I renounce the agreement that I am a victim." "I renounce the agreement that my body is dirty." "I renounce the agreement that I am defined by my past." "I renounce the agreement that I must repeat the patterns of my bloodline."

When you renounce, you are not asking for forgiveness. You are declaring independence. You are notifying the enemy that the contract is void, the portal is closed, and he no longer has legal access to your life.

Return the Property

Every unholy covenant comes with baggage. Emotional debt. Spiritual entanglement. Generational trauma that was never yours to carry in the first place. And as long as you're holding onto it, as long as you're carrying the shame, the bitterness, the unforgiveness, the identity that someone else gave you, you are still tethered.

You must give it back.

Not to the person. To God. You must lay it at the altar and say,

"This was never mine. I release it. I return it to the one who gave it to me, and I refuse to carry it any longer."

This is why forgiveness is so critical to sexual healing. Not because the person deserves it. But because unforgiveness is a tether. It keeps the portal open. It keeps you bound to the very thing you're trying to leave.

Change Your Name

In the Bible, a name change signifies a covenant shift. Abram becomes Abraham. Sarai becomes Sarah. Jacob becomes Israel. Simon becomes Peter. The old identity is buried, and a new one is declared.

You are no longer "The Addict." You are no longer "The Divorced One." You are no longer "The Victim" or "The Mistake" or "The One Who Can't Get It Right."

You are the Redeemed. The Restored. The One Who Left Egypt. The One Who Closed the Portal. The One Who Severed the Tie.

Your past does not get to name you. Your bloodline does not get to define you. The Cultural Parents do not get to write your identity. God does. And He has already declared who you are: beloved, whole, free, and fully His.

Moving Toward the Cleave

Leaving is the Exodus. Cleaving is the Inhabitation.

You are clearing the land so that God can build a new temple. You are demolishing the old altars so that a holy fire can burn on ground that was always meant to be sacred. You are severing the ties so that when you finally cleave to a spouse, to God, to your true identity, there is nothing pulling you backward.

This is hard work. It is painful work. It requires you to sit in the Wilderness longer than you want to. It requires you to divorce voices that have been with you since childhood. It requires you to sign a bill of divorcement for agreements you didn't even know you'd made.

But it is the only way forward.

Because until the old structures are demolished, the new glory has nowhere to rest. Until the Cultural Parents are evicted, the Seventh Man cannot move in. Until you leave, you cannot cleave.

The Woman at the Well left her waterpot. She left her shame. She left her identity as "The One with Five Husbands." And when she did, she became the first evangelist of her city. Her wound became her witness. Her past became her platform.

The same is waiting for you. But first, you have to be willing to leave.

The Seventh Man is calling. The Promised Land is ahead. But you cannot carry Egypt with you. It's time to sign the divorce papers. It's time to sever the ties. It's time to leave.

Chapter 5:

The Generational Portals

How Iniquity Travels Through The Bloodline Via Sexual Gateways

Chapter 5: The Power of Cleaving

The Divine Art of Spiritual Fusion

You have left. You have signed the divorce papers. You have severed the ties to the Cultural Parents, closed the portals, and walked through the Wilderness of the Soul. The old structures are demolished. The ground is cleared. The silence has done its work.

Now comes the part everyone has been waiting for: the cleaving.

"For this cause shall a man leave father and mother and shall cleave to his wife: and they twain shall be one flesh" (Matthew 19:5).

We love this verse. We quote it at weddings. We frame it on bedroom walls. We use it to justify why sex matters and why marriage is sacred. But most people skip over the most important detail: cleaving only works if you've done the leaving first.

You cannot cleave to something new while you're still tethered to something old. You cannot fuse two metals together if one of them is still corroded. You cannot create harmonic resonance if one instrument is still out of tune.

Cleaving is not about two broken people clinging to each other for survival. It is about two whole people creating a frequency so powerful that it opens a portal to the divine. It is about spiritual fusion. It is about becoming one new entity that the enemy cannot penetrate and the generations cannot ignore. This is what God designed. This is what the enemy has been trying to counterfeit since the Garden. And this is what you are now ready to step into, if you understand the mechanics.

Cleaving Is Not Codependency

Let's be clear about what cleaving is not. Cleaving is not two people using each other to fill the voids left by their unhealed trauma. It is not a woman looking for a man to validate her worth. It is not a man looking for a woman to manage his shame. It is not two people merging their dysfunction and calling it intimacy.

That's not cleaving. That's codependency. And codependency is a counterfeit covenant—a false fusion that looks like intimacy but is actually two people drowning together.

Codependency says: "I need you to complete me." Cleaving says: "I am whole, and so are you. Let's create something greater than the sum of our parts."

Codependency is need-based. Cleaving is frequency-based.

When two people cleave in the biblical sense, they are not filling each other's deficits. They harmonize their frequencies. They are tuning their spirits to the same divine pitch so that when they come together, physically, emotionally, spiritually, they create a resonance that amplifies the presence of God.

This is why the Woman at the Well had to encounter the Seventh Man before she could experience true intimacy. She had to become whole first. She had to stop looking for a man to complete her and start looking to Jesus to restore her. And when she did, when she left her waterpot and her shame, and her identity as "The One with Five Husbands", she became a well herself. She became a source, not a drain.

This is the prerequisite for cleaving: you must be whole first. Not perfect. Not sinless. But whole. Healed enough that you're not looking for someone to rescue you. Free enough that you're not trying to rescue someone else. Clear enough that your frequency is no longer distorted by the static of unhealed covenants.

Because when two whole people cleave, they don't just create intimacy. They create power.

The Dabeq Frequency: What God Actually Designed

The English word "cleave" is a contronym; it can mean to split apart (like a meat cleaver) or to stick together. But the Hebrew word used in Genesis 2:24 is Dabeq. Dabeq doesn't mean to stand next to someone. It doesn't mean having a contract with them. It doesn't mean to tolerate them or manage them or negotiate with them.

Dabeq means to be impeded. To be glued. To be fused. In modern terms, it's like two pieces of metal being welded together until the seam disappears. It's like two frequencies harmonizing so perfectly that they create a third tone, a resonance that neither could produce alone. This is what God designed sex to be: a spiritual welding. A frequency fusion. A divine act where two people, body, soul, and spirit, become one new entity.

And here's the key: this fusion happens on multiple levels simultaneously.

The Asa (Physical) Cleave: Your bodies become a sanctuary of mutual pleasure, vulnerability, and procreation. This is the part everyone focuses on. The chemistry. The attraction. The physical union. But this is only the surface level.

The Bara (Spiritual) Cleave: Your spirits create a fortress that generational habits cannot penetrate. When two people cleave in covenant, their combined spiritual frequency creates a protective barrier around their union. The enemy can attack from the outside, but he cannot breach the fortress. The

Cultural Parents can whisper from a distance, but they cannot enter the bedroom. The Ancestral Altars can demand repetition, but they have no legal access.

This is why the enemy fights the marriage bed so fiercely. He's not just trying to make you "sin." He's trying to prevent the fusion. Because when two people Dabeq correctly, when they cleave in the presence of God, with clean portals and healed bloodlines, they become a generational weapon. They don't just experience intimacy. They shift atmospheres. They heal bloodlines. They open portals to heaven rather than to hell. They become a living testimony that the enemy's system is a lie, and God's design is unstoppable.

The Generational Portal You're Opening

Here's what most people don't understand about holy sex: it doesn't just affect you. It affects your entire bloodline, past, present, and future. When you cleave in covenant, you are opening a generational portal. But unlike the portals opened by unholy unions, this portal flows in two directions: it heals up, and it blesses down.

Healing Up: When you break the cycle of sexual dysfunction in your generation, you are retroactively closing portals that have been open for decades, maybe centuries. You are standing in the gap for your parents, your grandparents, your great-grandparents, as well as everyone who came before you and couldn't break free. You are saying, "The curse stops here. The pattern ends with me. I am closing the door that you couldn't close, and I am healing the wound that you couldn't heal."

This is why your healing journey is so important. It's not just about you. It's about your entire lineage. Every time you renounce an unholy covenant, you are cutting a tether that has been binding on your bloodline for generations. Every time you close a portal, you are locking a door that your ancestors left open. Every time you cleave in holiness, you are rewriting the spiritual DNA of your family tree.

Blessing Down: When you cleave in covenant, you are also opening a portal of blessing for your children, your grandchildren, and every generation that comes after you. You are creating a spiritual inheritance. You are establishing a frequency that they will inherit. You are building a fortress that they will grow inside.

This is why children raised in homes where the parents have a healthy, holy, covenant-based sexual relationship tend to have healthier relationships themselves. It's not just about what they see. It's about what they inherit. It's about the frequency they absorb. It's about the portal that was opened over their lives before they were even born.

Your cleaving is not just about your pleasure. It's about your legacy. It's about the generations that will come after you and inherit the frequency you establish today.

The Three Seasons of Cleaving

Cleaving is not a one-time event. It is a process. A journey. A progression through three distinct seasons, each with its own purpose and its own challenges.

Season One: The Courtship of Self

This is the season you're in right now. The season of leaving. The season of healing. The season of becoming whole. You are courting yourself. You are learning to love the person God created you to be. You are discovering your frequency, your identity, your worth, not based on who wants you but based on who God says you are.

This season is not about finding someone. It's about becoming someone. It's about doing the inner work so that when the time comes to cleave, you're not bringing your brokenness into the union. You're bringing your wholeness.

This is the season where you close the portals. Where you divorce the Cultural Parents. Where you sit in the Wilderness and let God clear the land. And it is the most important season of all, because everything that comes after it depends on the work you do here.

Season Two: The Courtship of Frequency

This is the season where you meet someone whose frequency matches yours. Not someone who completes you. Not someone who fills your voids. But someone who resonates with you.

You know you've entered this season when you meet someone, and it doesn't feel like work. It doesn't feel like you're trying to convince them to love you or trying to fix them or trying to manage their dysfunction. It feels harmonious. Like two instruments tuned to the same pitch, creating a sound that neither could produce alone.

This is the season of discernment. Of testing the frequency. Of asking the hard questions: Is this person whole? Have they done the leaving work? Are their portals closed? Are they walking in freedom, or are they still tethered to the Five? Because here's the truth: you cannot clever yourself to someone who hasn't left. You cannot fuse with someone who is still corroded. You cannot create harmonic resonance with someone who is still out of tune.

This season requires patience. It requires wisdom. It requires the willingness to walk away if the frequency doesn't match, no matter how much you want it to work.

Season Three: The Sealed Covenant

This is the season of marriage. The season of Dabeq. The season where two whole people, with matching frequencies and clean portals, stand before God and declare: "We are one."

This is the season where the fusion happens. Where the welding occurs. Where the fortress is built. Where the generational portal is opened, and the blessing begins to flow. But here's the key: this season only works if you've done the work in the first two seasons. If you skip the Courtship of Self, you bring brokenness into the union. If you skip the Courtship of Frequency, you marry someone who doesn't resonate with you. And if you do either of those things, the Sealed Covenant becomes a prison instead of paradise.

God's design is sequential. Leaving, then cleaving. Wholeness, then fusion. Frequency match, then covenant seal.

You cannot rush this process. You cannot skip steps. You cannot force the fusion before the frequencies are aligned.

But when you do it right, when you honor the seasons and trust the process, the result is unstoppable.

The Currency of the Covenant

Once you're in the Sealed Covenant season, there is a daily maintenance required to keep the frequency aligned. Because cleaving is not a one-time event. It is a continuous act of tuning, adjusting, and harmonizing. And here's where most marriages fail: they don't understand the currency.

Every covenant has a currency, a form of exchange that keeps the union healthy. In the marriage covenant, the currency is different for men and women. Not because one is more important than the other, but because God designed us with different frequencies that require different forms of fuel.

For the Wife: The Currency of Conversation

To a woman, cleaving often begins in the soul. She requires the "living water" of communication, emotional safety, and being truly seen. When a husband neglects the conversation, when he treats her like a body instead of a person, when he rushes past her heart to get to her body, he is effectively "un-gluing" the connection that makes physical intimacy holy. The "55s" start to look appealing again. For her, she is lured by the desire to be heard.

This is why so many women shut down sexually. It's not because they don't desire intimacy. It's because the frequency is off. The conversation has stopped. The emotional connection has been severed. And without that connection, sex feels like a transaction instead of a fusion.

A woman's body is a sanctuary, and the door to that sanctuary is her heart. If you want access to the sanctuary, you must honor the door.

For the Husband: The Currency of Fulfillment

To a man, cleaving is often validated through physical union and respect. It is his "point of contact" with the covenant. It is how he experiences the fusion, how he feels connected, how he knows that the frequency is aligned.

When this is withheld, when sex is treated as a chore, a reward, or a weapon, his sense of "oneness" begins to erode. He starts to feel rejected, disconnected, and undesired. And in that vulnerability, he becomes susceptible to the "Hyper-Sexual Delusions" we discussed in Chapter 1. The "55s" start to look appealing again. The Cultural Parents start to whisper again. The old portals start to crack open again. A man's spirit is a fortress, and the fuel for that fortress is honor. If you want him to protect the covenant, you must honor the covenant.

The Balance

Here's the key: both currencies must flow. Conversation without fulfillment creates resentment. Fulfillment without conversation creates emptiness. But when both currencies are honored, when the wife receives the emotional connection she needs, and the husband receives the physical intimacy he needs, the frequency aligns. The fusion deepens. The covenant strengthens.

This is not about keeping score. It's not about "I did this, so you owe me that." It's about understanding that God designed us with different frequencies, and those frequencies require different forms of fuel. When we honor the design, the union thrives. When we ignore it, the union dies.

The Third Cord: The Seventh Man in the Marriage Bed

But here's the most important part: true cleaving is impossible without the presence of the Holy Spirit. Ecclesiastes 4:12 tells us that "a threefold cord is not quickly broken." Two people can create intimacy. But two people plus God create invincibility.

This is the Seventh Man encounter in the context of marriage. Just as the Woman at the Well needed Jesus to complete her, your marriage needs Jesus to sanctify it. He is the third chord. The divine frequency. The one who holds the fusion together when everything else is trying to pull it apart.

When a man and woman cleave in the presence of Jesus, they aren't just joining their broken histories. They are joining their redeemed futures. They aren't just merging their bloodlines. They are creating a new bloodline, one that flows from the throne of God instead of the altars of their ancestors.

This is why prayer matters in marriage. Why worship matters. Why inviting the Holy Spirit into your bedroom is not weird, it's essential. Because without Him, you're just two people trying to hold it together. But with Him, you're a fortress. A weapon. A generational portal of blessing.

The Seventh Man doesn't come to take. He comes to sanctify. He comes to seal the covenant. He comes to turn your union into a living testimony that God's design is real, powerful, and unstoppable.

The Frequency You're Creating

You are not just having sex. You are creating a frequency.

You are not just building a marriage. You are opening a portal.

You are not just experiencing intimacy. You are shifting atmospheres, healing bloodlines, and establishing a legacy that will outlive you.

This is what cleaving is. This is what God designed. This is what the enemy has been trying to counterfeit since the beginning.

And now that you understand the mechanics, now that you've

done the leaving, closed the portals, and aligned your frequency, you are ready to step into it.

The Seventh Man is waiting. The covenant is calling. The fusion is possible. But it requires patience. It requires wisdom. It requires the willingness to honor the seasons and trust the process.

The work you've done in the first four chapters has prepared you for this moment. The 30-day journey that follows will give you the practical tools to maintain this frequency, to protect this covenant, and to walk in the fullness of what God has designed for you.

You are not a victim of your past. You are not defined by the Five. You are not disqualified because of your history. You are whole. You are free. You are ready to cleave. The Seventh Man is in the room. The frequency is aligned. The portal is open. Let the fusion begin.

Chapter 6:
The Ritual of the Soul

The Five-Step Cycle of Pain and How to Interrupt the Moment of Addiction

Chapter 6: The Ritual of the Soul

Exposing the Mechanics of Strongholds

For many, sexual struggle feels like an unpredictable storm; it just "happens." But the Holy Spirit is a God of order, and the enemy, in his imitation, is a spirit of ritual. Your struggle isn't random; it is a sophisticated, repetitive cycle designed to keep your Bara (spirit) enslaved to your Asa (flesh).

To break the cycle, you must first understand its anatomy. Based on the patterns of the soul, we can trace the "Five Stations of the Stronghold."

The Anatomy of the Cycle

The Trigger (The Pain): It always begins with a deficit. It might be loneliness, a sense of failure at work, or a "55" (a cultural seed) planted in your mind. This is the moment your soul feels "un-cleaved" and vulnerable.

The Fantasy (The Escape): Before the act comes the image. You begin to "re-build" a portal in your mind. This is where you start to negotiate with the "Cultural Parents" we discussed in Chapter 4.

The Ritual (The Grooming): This is the most dangerous phase. It is the set of behaviors that lead up to the act, browsing a certain site, driving a certain route, or sending a specific "innocent" text. The ritual "grooms" your brain for the dopamine hit.

The Acting Out (The Portal): The physical union or act. This is where the Asa takes total control and the spiritual portal is flung wide open.

The Shame (The Tether): After the act, the enemy switches from "Seducer" to "Accuser." Shame is the "glue" that hardens the cycle, making you feel too "dirty" to go to God, which ensures you stay in the pain... starting the cycle all over again.

Breaking the Cycle at the Root

You've done the diagnostic work. You've identified the Five Husbands. You've signed the divorce papers and walked through the Wilderness. You understand the mechanics of cleaving and the power of the Dabeq frequency. You know what God designed. You know what the enemy counterfeited. You know the difference between a portal to heaven and a portal to hell. But here's the problem: knowing the mechanics don't automatically stop the cycle.

Because sexual sin, whether it's pornography, fantasy, affairs, or compulsive behavior, is not just a moral failure. It's a ritual. A deeply ingrained pattern that has carved neural pathways in your brain and spiritual grooves in your soul. It has a rhythm. A sequence. A momentum that builds like a freight train until it feels unstoppable.

And here's where most people fail: they try to fight the battle at the wrong stage. They wait until they're already in the act, until the portal is already open, the dopamine is already flooding, the Asa is already in control, and then they try to stop. They white-knuckle it. They pray in the moment. They beg God to take away the desire while their hand is already reaching for the phone, their feet are already walking toward the door, their mind is already deep in the fantasy. But by then, the spiritual momentum is like a freight train. You're not fighting temptation anymore. You're fighting inertia. And inertia almost always wins.

This is why so many people cycle through the same pattern over and over again. They repent on Sunday, fall on Tuesday, repent again on Wednesday, fall again on Friday. They feel like failures. They wonder if they're too broken to be healed. They start to believe the lie that they'll never be free.

But the problem isn't that you're too broken. The problem is that you're fighting the wrong battle at the wrong stage.

Victory is not won at the moment of acting out. Victory is won at the moment of fantasy. At first thought. At the first image. At the first whisper of the "55" trying to rebuild the portal in your mind.

This is where the battle must be fought. This is where the cycle must be broken. This is where you reclaim authority over your own soul.

The Anatomy of the Cycle

Before we can break the cycle, we need to understand its anatomy. Because the enemy doesn't just tempt you randomly. He follows a pattern. A ritual. A sequence of stages that builds momentum until the acting out feels inevitable.

Here's how it works:

Stage 1: The Trigger (The Pain)

It always begins with a deficit. A void. A moment where your soul feels "un-cleaved" and vulnerable.

Maybe it's loneliness. Maybe it's a sense of failure at work. Maybe it's rejection from your spouse. Maybe it's boredom. Maybe it's exhaustion. Maybe it's just the weight of life pressing down on you, and you don't know how to carry it.

This is the moment the enemy has been waiting for. Because pain creates a vacuum. And vacuums demand to be filled.

This is where the "55s" from Chapter 1 comes back into play. The cultural seeds that were planted in your subconscious years ago suddenly start to sprout. The images you saw. The messages you absorbed. The lies you believed about what will make you feel better, what will fill the void, what will ease the pain.

The trigger is not the sin. The trigger is the opportunity. It's the crack in the door. The moment of vulnerability where the enemy whispers, "I know what will make you feel better."

Stage 2: The Fantasy (The Escape)

Before the act comes the image. Before the portal opens in reality, it opens in your mind. This is where you begin to "re-build" the portal. You start to entertain the thought. You start to negotiate with the Cultural Parents we discussed in Chapter 4. You start to tell yourself the lies: "Just this once." "It's not that bad." "I deserve this." "No one will know." "I'll stop after this time."

The fantasy is the blueprint. It's the architectural plan for the portal you're about to open. And here's the key: the fantasy is where spiritual battle is actually happening. Because once the fantasy takes root, once the image becomes vivid, once the negotiation is complete, the acting out is almost inevitable.

This is why 2 Corinthians 10:5 is so critical: "Casting down imaginations, and every high thing that exalteth itself against the knowledge of God and bringing into captivity every thought to the obedience of Christ."

Paul didn't say "cast down actions." He said "cast down imaginations." Because he understood that the battle is won or lost in the mind. The fantasy is the seed. The acting out is just the harvest.

Stage 3: The Ritual (The Grooming)

This is the most dangerous phase, and it's the one most people don't recognize. The ritual is the set of behaviors that lead up to the act. It's the "grooming" process, not of another person, but of yourself. You are grooming your own brain for the dopamine hit. You are creating the conditions for the portal to open.

Maybe it's browsing a certain website "just to look." Maybe it's driving a certain route past a certain place. Maybe it's sending a "harmless" text to someone you know you shouldn't be texting. Maybe it's staying up late when everyone else is asleep. Maybe it's taking your phone into the bedroom. Maybe it's pouring that second drink. Maybe it's scrolling through social media until the images start to blur together and the "55s" start to feel normal.

The ritual is insidious because it feels innocent. It feels like you're not doing anything wrong yet. You're just... preparing. You're just... setting the stage. You're just... creating the opportunity.

But here's the truth: the ritual is the sin. The moment you start the grooming process, you've already opened the door. You've already given the enemy legal access. You've already started the freight train down the tracks.

Stage 4: Acting Out (The Portal)

This is the moment everyone focuses on. The physical union. The click of the mouse. The meeting in the hotel room. The moment when the Asa takes total control and the spiritual portal is flung wide open.

But by the time you get here, the battle is already over. The fantasy has taken root. The ritual has groomed your brain. The momentum is unstoppable. You're no longer making a choice. You're just following the script.

This is why fighting at this stage is so exhausting. Because you're not fighting temptation. You're fighting inevitability. And inevitability doesn't lose.

Stage 5: The Shame (The Tether)

After the act, the enemy switches roles. He goes from Seducer to Accuser. From "This will make you feel better" to "Look what you've done. You're disgusting. You're hopeless. You'll never be free."

Shame is the glue that hardens the cycle. It's the tether that keeps you bound. Because shame makes you feel too dirty to go to God. Too broken to be healed. Too far gone to be restored.

And so you stay in the pain. You carry the weight. You hide the secret. And the next time the trigger comes, the next time you feel lonely, rejected, exhausted, or empty, the cycle starts all over again.

This is the anatomy of the ritual. This is the pattern the enemy uses to keep you enslaved. And this is why most people never break free: they're fighting at Stage 4 when the battle was already lost at Stage 2.

Interrupting the Fantasy: High-Frequency Warfare

If the battle is won or lost at the fantasy stage, then that's where we must learn to fight.

This is what Paul calls "casting down imaginations." In the Charismatic tradition, we call it High-Frequency Warfare. Because the fantasy is not just a thought. It's a frequency. It's a spiritual signal trying to tune your soul to the enemy's station.

And the only way to interrupt a frequency is to replace it with a higher frequency.

This is where the "55s" meet the "7." The world's seed meets

God's Word. The enemy's whisper meets the Holy Spirit's roar.

When the fantasy begins, when the first image flashes in your mind, when the first thought whispers, "This will make you feel better", you have a choice. You can entertain it, or you can cast it down.

Casting down is not passive. It's not just ignoring the thought and hoping it goes away. It's an active, aggressive, violent act of spiritual warfare. It's grabbing the thought by the throat and throwing it out of your mind before it can take root.

And here's how you do it: you replace the "55" with the "7."

The moment the fantasy begins, you speak the Word. Out loud if you have to. You declare the truth over the lie. You tune your frequency to God's station instead of the enemy's.

"I am the righteousness of God in Christ Jesus." (2 Corinthians 5:21)

"Greater is He that is in me than he that is in the world." (1 John 4:4)

"I have been crucified with Christ; it is no longer I who live, but Christ who lives in me." (Galatians 2:20)

"No weapon formed against me shall prosper." (Isaiah 54:17)

These are not just nice verses. These are weapons. These

are frequencies. These are the "7s" that dismantle the "55s" before they can build a stronghold. Because here's the key: thoughts become strongholds. Fantasies become fortresses. If you let the image sit in your mind for five minutes, it becomes a thought. If you let the thought sit for five hours, it becomes a plan. If you let the plan sit for five days, it becomes an action. And if you let the action repeat for five weeks, it becomes a stronghold.

But if you cast it down at the fantasy stage, if you interrupt the frequency before it can build momentum, you stop the cycle before it starts. This is High-Frequency Warfare. This is the battle that most people never learn to fight. And this is why so many people stay enslaved: they're trying to tear down strongholds when they should have been casting down imaginations.

Starving the Ritual: Closing the Door Before the Spirit Arrives

But interrupting the fantasy is only half the battle. Because fantasies don't exist in a vacuum. They need grooming behaviors to survive. They need rituals to feed them. They need conditions to thrive. This is where you must become ruthlessly practical.

You must identify your grooming behaviors. You must

recognize the rituals that precede the acting out. And you must starve them.

If the ritual starts with your phone in bed, the phone must stay in the kitchen. If the ritual starts with late-night isolation, you must create accountability. If the ritual starts with certain websites, you must install blockers. If the ritual starts with certain routes, you must drive a different way. If the ritual starts with certain people, you must cut off contact.

This is not legalism. This is wisdom. This is recognizing that you are not just fighting a spiritual battle, you are fighting a physical battle. The Asa and the Bara are connected. What you do with your body affects what happens in your spirit. And what happens in your spirit affects what you do with your body. You are physically closing the door before the spirit arrives.

Think of it this way: if you knew a thief was planning to break into your house at midnight, would you leave the front door unlocked? Would you leave the windows open? Would you put a welcome mat on the porch? Of course not. You would lock the doors. You would close the windows. You would turn on the lights. You would make it as hard as possible for the thief to get in.

This is what you're doing with your grooming behaviors.

You're locking the doors. You're closing the windows. You're making it as hard as possible for the enemy to get in. Because here's the truth: the enemy is lazy. He's not going to work harder than he has to. If you make it difficult for him to access you, he'll move on to an easier target. But if you leave the door open, if you keep the phone in the bedroom, if you keep scrolling late at night, if you keep entertaining the fantasy, he'll walk right in.

Starving the ritual is not about willpower. It's about strategy. It's about recognizing the patterns and dismantling them before they can build momentum.

From Ritual to Liturgy: Replacing Death with Life

But here's the most important part: you cannot just stop a ritual. You must replace it. Because the pain that triggers the cycle is real. The loneliness is real. The rejection is real. The exhaustion is real. The void is real.

And if you don't fill the void with something, it will fill itself with the same thing it always has. This is why white-knuckle discipline never works. This is why "just say no" is not a strategy. This is why most people who try to quit cold turkey relapse within weeks.

Because you're not just breaking a Death Ritual. You're trying to live without a ritual at all. And the soul cannot survive without a ritual. The soul needs a rhythm. A pattern. A liturgy. The only way to permanently break a Death Ritual is to replace it with a Life Liturgy.

When the pain hits, when the loneliness comes, when the rejection stings, when the exhaustion weighs you down, you must have a new ritual. A new pattern. A new response.

Instead of turning to the fantasy, you turn to the Seventh Man. Instead of seeking Acting Out of the Flesh, you seek the Conversation of Prayer. Instead of opening a portal to hell, you open a portal to heaven.

This is Life Liturgy. This is the new rhythm. This is the sustainable path to freedom.

And here's what it looks like practically:

When the trigger comes, you don't ignore it. You don't suppress it. You don't pretend you're not in pain. You acknowledge it. You name it. You bring it into the light.

"I feel lonely right now." "I feel rejected right now." "I feel exhausted right now." "I feel empty right now." And then you turn toward God instead of away from Him.

You pray. You worship. You read the Word. You call a friend. You go for a walk. You journal. You do whatever it takes to redirect the pain toward the Healer instead of toward the counterfeit.

This is not about being perfect. This is not about never feeling pain. This is about redirecting the pain toward the One who can heal it, rather than toward the one who will only deepen it.

The Death Ritual says: "This pain is unbearable. I need relief now. I'll do whatever it takes to make it stop."

The Life Liturgy says: "This pain is real. But I know the One who can carry it. And I'm going to bring it to Him instead of burying it in sin." This is the transformation. This is the shift. This is the moment when you stop being a slave to the cycle and start becoming a steward of your own soul.

The Authority You're Reclaiming

Here's what you need to understand: this is not about white-knuckle discipline. This is not about trying harder. This is not about being strong enough to resist temptation. This is about reclaiming authority over your own soul.

For too long, you've been a passenger in your own life. The cycle has been driving. The ritual has been in control. The enemy has been calling the shots.

But when you interrupt the fantasy, when you starve the ritual, when you replace the Death Ritual with a Life Liturgy, you are taking back the wheel. You are reclaiming the authority that God gave you from the beginning.

You are no longer a slave to the cycle. You are a son. A daughter. A co-heir with Christ. A carrier of the Holy Spirit. A temple of the living God. And the enemy has no legal right to your soul unless you give it to him. This is the authority you're reclaiming. This is the power you're stepping into. This is the freedom that Jesus died to give you.

"If the Son therefore shall make you free, ye shall be free indeed" (John 8:36).

Not free from temptation. Not free from pain. But free from the cycle. Free from the ritual. Free from the slavery of acting out every time the trigger comes.

You are free to choose a different path. You are free to build a different rhythm. You are free to create a Life Liturgy that leads to healing instead of a Death Ritual that leads to shame.

This is the authority you're reclaiming. And it starts today.

The Altar Awaits

The work you've done in these six chapters has prepared you for this moment. You understand the mechanics. You've identified the Five. You've signed the divorce papers. You've walked through the Wilderness. You understand the power of cleaving. And now you understand how to break the cycle at the root.

But understanding is not enough. Knowledge is not transformation. You must practice what you've learned. You must build Life Liturgy. You must create a new rhythm. You must establish the new pattern. This is where the 30-Day Workbook comes in. This is where the theory becomes practice. This is where the teaching becomes transformation.

The workbook is not a list of rules. It's not a set of religious obligations. It's not about trying harder or being more disciplined.

It's about building an altar. A daily place where you meet with the Seventh Man. A daily rhythm where you practice Life Liturgy. A daily pattern where you interrupt the fantasy, starve the ritual, and redirect the pain toward the Healer.

This is the altar of restoration. This is where the cycle is broken. This is where the frequency is aligned. This is where the portal to heaven stays open, and the portal to hell stays closed.

The Seventh Man is waiting. The altar is prepared. The Life Liturgy is ready to be built.

It's time to step into the daily practice of freedom.

Let's continue.

PART III: THE PATHWAY TO RESTORATION

Chapter 7:

The Art of Leaving and Cleaving

Severing Ties With 'Culture Parents' and Signing the Spiritual Bill of Divorcement

Chapter 7: The Altar of Restoration

From Secret Shame to Public Power

The story of the Samaritan woman does not end at the well.

Most people think the miracle happened when Jesus told her everything she had ever done. They think the transformation occurred when she recognized Him as the Messiah. They think the healing was complete when she received the living water.

But that was only the beginning.

The real miracle; the one that proves the portal has been cleansed, the frequency has shifted, and the cycle has been broken, happens in John 4:28-29: "The woman then left her waterpot, and went her way into the city, and saith to the men, Come, see a man, which told me all things that ever I did: is not this the Christ?"

Notice what she left behind: her waterpot.

The very thing that represented her thirst. Her labor. Her shame. Her daily ritual of coming to the well at noon to avoid the judgment of the other women. The symbol of her old cycle, the endless drawing of water that never satisfied, the endless search for something to fill the void. She left it at the well. Because she didn't need it anymore. She had become a well herself.

This is the moment where secret shame transforms into public power. This is the moment when the healed portal becomes a weapon. This is the moment where the woman who hid in the shadows at noon walks boldly into the city in broad daylight and says to the very men who knew her history, "Come and see."

She didn't hide her past. She didn't minimize it. She didn't say, "Come see a man who told me some things." She said, "Come see a man who told me all things that ever I did."

Her scars became her credentials. Her history became her testimony. Her shame became her authority. And the city was shaken. John 4:39 says, "And many of the Samaritans of that city believed on him for the saying of the woman, which testified, He told me all that ever I did."

This is what happens when the portal is cleansed. This is what happens when the frequency shifts. This is what happens when you stop hiding and start testifying.

Your restoration doesn't just heal you. It provokes a city.

The Cleansed Portal: When God Sanctifies Your History

When God heals your sexual history, He doesn't just "forgive and forget." He doesn't just wipe the slate clean and pretend it never happened. He doesn't just cover your shame with grace and move on.

He sanctifies the portal.

He takes the very thing the enemy used to destroy you, the very doorway that was opened to hell, the very covenant that bound you to generational habits, the very frequency that kept you enslaved—and He transforms it into a weapon.

Your past becomes your most powerful evidence. Your scars become proof of the Surgeon's skill. Your testimony becomes what sets other captives free.

This is what Paul means in 2 Corinthians 1:3-4: "Blessed be God, even the Father of our Lord Jesus Christ, the Father of mercies, and the God of all comfort; Who comforteth us in all our tribulation, that we may be able to comfort them which are in any trouble, by the comfort wherewith we ourselves are comforted of God."

God doesn't waste your pain. He doesn't throw away your history. He doesn't erase your story. He redeems it. He sanctifies it. He weaponizes it. The portal that was once opened to the Five Husbands, the portal that allowed shame, lust, rejection, trauma, and generational habits to flood your soul, is now cleansed by the Blood of the Lamb. And when the Blood sanctifies a portal, it doesn't just close it. It reverses it.

Now, instead of a doorway for the enemy to enter, it becomes a doorway for the Holy Spirit to flow out. Instead of a place of shame, it becomes a place of authority. Instead of a wound that weakens you, it becomes a scar that strengthens others.

This is the cleansed portal. This is what happens when the Seventh Man touches your history. This is why your testimony is so powerful.

Because when people look at you—when they see your freedom, your wholeness, your peace, your joy—they don't just see someone who "got lucky" or "had it easier." They see someone who was just as broken as they are and yet somehow found a way out.

And that provokes them. It shakes them. It makes them ask the same question the Samaritans asked: "Is not this the Christ?"

Your cleansed portal becomes the evidence that Jesus is real. That healing is possible. That the cycle can be broken. The frequency can shift. That the Five Husbands can be divorced and the Seventh Man can be received.

This is the power of sanctified history. This is why God doesn't erase your past. He transforms it into your greatest weapon.

From "Recovering" to "New Creation"

But here's where most people get stuck: they live in the identity of "recovering" instead of "restored." They say things like, "I'm a recovering sex addict." "I'm a victim of past trauma." "I'm working on my issues." "I'm trying to get better."

And while there's nothing wrong with acknowledging the journey, there's a massive problem with making the journey your identity.

Because the moment you define yourself by what you're recovering from, you're still giving the Five Husbands authority over your soul. You're still vibrating at the frequency of your past instead of the frequency of your future. You're still seeing yourself through the lens of shame instead of the lens of the Blood.

This is not who you are.

2 Corinthians 5:17 says, "Therefore if any man be in Christ, he is a new creature: old things are passed away; behold, all things are become new." Not "becoming" new. Not "working toward" new. Not "recovering into" new. Become new. Past tense. Done. Finished. Complete.

When God looks at your portal in the Spirit, He doesn't see the Five Husbands. He doesn't see your history. He doesn't see shame, the trauma, the cycles, the failures, the relapses, the wounds. He sees the Blood of the Covenant.

He sees the Seventh Man standing in the doorway, guarding the portal, sanctifying the space, declaring over you: "This one is Mine. This one is clean. This one is whole. This one is a New Creation." And if that's how God sees you, that's how you must learn to see yourself. This is not denial. This is not pretending the past didn't happen. This is not "fake it till you make it" positive thinking. This is a spiritual reality. This is the truth of what happened the moment you renounced the Five, walked through the Wilderness, and cleaved to the Seventh Man. You were re-created. You were reborn. You were re-covenanted.

The old portal was closed. The new portal was opened. The old frequency was silenced. The new frequency was activated. You are not recovering. You are restored. You are not a victim. You are a victor. You are not broken. You are whole.

And the moment you start walking in that identity—the moment you start speaking from that frequency, thinking from that reality, living from that truth, everything changes. Because identity determines authority. And authority determines what you allow into your life and what you keep out.

When you see yourself as "recovering," you're still giving the enemy permission to knock on the door. You're still entertained by the possibility of relapse. You're still vibrating at the frequency of "maybe I'll fall again." But when you see yourself as a New Creation, when you stand in the authority of the Blood, when you declare the truth of who you are in Christ, when you walk in the identity of the sanctified portal, the enemy has no legal right to your soul.

The door is closed. The portal is guarded. The frequency is locked in. You are whole. And wholeness is not a destination. It's a declaration.

Testimony as Weaponized Evidence

Revelation 12:11 says, "And they overcame him by the blood of the Lamb, and by the word of their testimony; and they loved not their lives unto the death." Notice the order: the Blood comes first. The testimony comes second. You cannot testify to something you haven't experienced. You cannot weaponize a story that isn't yours. You cannot provoke a city with secondhand information.

But when the Blood has sanctified your portal, when the

Seventh Man has healed your history, when the Five Husbands have been divorced, when the frequency has shifted, when the cycle has been broken, your testimony becomes a weapon. Not just a story. Not just a "share." Not just a "testimony time" at church.

A weapon. A tool of warfare. A piece of spiritual artillery that dismantles strongholds, breaks chains, and sets captives free.

Because when you testify, when you stand up and say, "I was bound, but now I'm free. I was enslaved, but now I'm whole. I was trapped in the cycle, but the Seventh Man broke it. I was vibrating at the frequency of the Five, but now I'm resonating with the frequency of the One." You're not just sharing information.

You're creating a frequent shift in the atmosphere. You're opening a portal for others to walk through. You're giving them permission to believe that if God did it for you, He can do it for them. You're proving that the cycle can be broken, the shame can be healed, the portal can be cleansed.

This is why the enemy fights so hard to keep you silent. This is why shame whispers, "Don't tell anyone. They'll judge you. They'll reject you. They'll think less of you." Because the enemy knows that the moment you open your mouth and testify to what the Blood has done, his power is broken. The lie is exposed. The stronghold crumbles.

Your testimony is not just your story. It's evidence. It's proof. It's a legal document in the courts of heaven that declares: "The Blood works. The Seventh Man heals. The portal can be cleansed. The cycle can be broken."

And when people hear that evidence, when they see your freedom, your wholeness, your peace, they start to believe it's possible for them too. This is how cities are shaken. This is how generations are healed. This is how the Kingdom advances.

Not through perfect people with perfect stories. But through broken people with sanctified scars who are willing to say, "Come and see what the Seventh Man did for me." Walking as a Portal of Blessing

But the power of your restoration doesn't just flow forward. It flows backward.

Remember what we discussed in Chapter 2: sexual sin opens a portal that flows in two directions. It opens downward to your descendants (cursing the generations that come after you), and it opens upward to your ancestors (binding you to the unhealed trauma and sin patterns of those who came before you).

But when the portal is cleansed, when the Blood sanctifies your history, when the Seventh Man heals your soul, when you walk in the authority of the New Creation, the flow reverses.

Now, instead of a portal that curses, you become a portal that blesses.

Your wholeness doesn't just heal you. It heals backward through your ancestral line. It breaks the generational habits that have been passed down for decades, maybe centuries. It closes the doors that your parents, grandparents, and great-grandparents left open. It silences the lies that have been whispering through your family tree for generations.

And it heals forward to your children and your children's children. It opens a doorway of blessing instead of a doorway of bondage. It establishes a new frequency in your lineage. It creates a new pattern, a new rhythm, a new legacy. This is what it means to be a generational healer instead of a generational habit carrier.

You are not just breaking the cycle for yourself. You are breaking it for everyone connected to you, past, present, and future. This is the power of the cleansed portal. This is the authority you're walking into. This is the legacy you're creating.

When you walk in wholeness, you don't just change your life. You change your lineage.

The Authority You're Walking In

Let's be clear about something: this is not arrogance. This is not pride. This is not you trying to be something you're not.

This is the legitimate reclamation of dominion. From the beginning, God gave humanity authority over the earth. Genesis 1:28 says, "And God blessed them, and God said unto them, Be fruitful, and multiply, and replenish the earth, and subdue it: and have dominion."

Dominion. Authority. Stewardship. The right to rule over your own soul, your own body, your own life. But when sin entered, when the portal was opened to the enemy, when the covenant was broken, when the frequency shifted, that authority was forfeited. The enemy gained legal access. The cycle took control. The Five Husbands moved in and started running the house. But when the Blood sanctifies the portal, when the Seventh Man heals your soul, when you renounce the Five and cleave to the One, you are reclaiming the authority that was always meant to be yours.

You have authority over your own soul now. Authority over the cycle. Authority over the frequency. Authority over which portals stay open and which stay closed.

This is not you trying to be God. This is you partnering with God. This is you stepping into the role He designed you for from the beginning: a steward of your own life, a guardian of your own soul, a gatekeeper of your own spirit. And when you walk in that authority, when you declare, "This portal is closed. This frequency is locked in. This cycle is broken. This covenant is sealed", the enemy has no choice but to obey.

Because you're not speaking from your own power. You're speaking from the authority of the Blood. You're declaring the truth of the New Creation. You're standing in the identity of the sanctified portal. And that authority is unshakable. Unbreakable. Unstoppable.

This is who you are now. This is the power you're walking in. This is the freedom you've been given. Don't shrink back from it. Don't apologize for it. Don't let shame or fear or the enemy's lies convince you that you're not worthy of it. You are a New Creation. You are a cleansed portal. You are a generational healer. You are a carrier of the Seventh Man's frequency.

Walk in it. Declare it. Live it.

The Altar of Restoration: Sealing the Covenant

If you are reading this and you are ready to seal your healing, if you are ready to step into the authority of the New Creation, to walk as a cleansed portal, to testify to what the Blood has done, then it's time to build the altar.

This is not just a prayer. This is a covenant. A declaration. A sealing of everything you've learned, everything you've renounced, everything you've received. This is the moment when you formally close the old portals and open the new one. Where you silence the frequency of the Five and lock in the frequency of the Seventh Man. Where you leave the waterpot at the well and walk into the city with your testimony. Pray this out loud. Declare it with authority. Seal it with the Blood.

The Covenant of Wholeness:

Heavenly Father, I come before You in the name of Jesus, the Seventh Man, the One who told me all things that ever I did and loved me anyway.

I thank You for the Blood of the Lamb that speaks better things than the blood of my past. I thank You that the Blood doesn't just cover my sin, it sanctifies my history, cleanses my portal, and transforms my shame into a weapon.

I formally and permanently close every unholy portal that was opened through sexual sin, trauma, fantasy, or generational iniquity. I renounce every "55" the world has planted in my soul. I divorce the Five Husbands, every false covenant, every unholy union, every spiritual entanglement that has kept me bound.

I sever the tethers to the Mother of Shame, the Father of Lust, and the Ancestral Altar. I break every generational habit that has traveled through my bloodline. I close the portal that flows backward to my ancestors and forward to my descendants, and I declare that from this day forward, I am a portal of blessing, not bondage.

Lord, I cleave, "Dabeq" to You. I weld my spirit to Yours. I align my frequency with the frequency of heaven. I receive Your living water, and I declare that I am no longer thirsty for the things of this world. I am satisfied in You.

I am not recovering. I am restored. I am not a victim. I am a victor. I am not broken. I am whole. I am a New Creation. Old things have passed away. All things have become new.

I take authority over my own soul. I am the gatekeeper of my spirit. I decide which portals stay open and which stay closed. I decide which frequencies I vibrate at and which I silence. I decide which covenants I honor and which I renounce.

And I declare that this portal is now sanctified. This frequency is now locked in. This cycle is now broken. This covenant is now sealed.

I am a carrier of the Seventh Man's presence. I am a generational healer. I am a weapon in the hands of God. My testimony is evidence. My scars are credentials. My freedom is a provocation to the city.

I leave my waterpot at the well. I walk into the city in broad daylight. I testify to what You have done. And I declare that many will believe because of the word of my testimony.

In the name of Jesus, the Seventh Man, the One who heals all things, I seal this covenant. Amen.

The Threshold: Stepping Into Daily Restoration

The altar is built. The covenant is sealed. The portal is cleansed. But here's the truth: restoration is not a one-time event. It's a daily practice.

The Woman at the Well didn't just have one encounter with Jesus and then coast for the rest of her life. She had to learn to draw from the well inside her rather than constantly returning to the well outside her. She had to learn to maintain the frequency. She had to learn to guard the portal. She had to learn to walk in the authority of her New Creation identity every single day.

This is where the 30-Day Workbook comes in.

The workbook is not "more work." It's not a list of religious obligations or a set of rules to follow. It's not about trying harder or being more disciplined. It's the daily maintenance of the altar. It's the practical, tangible, lived-out expression of everything you've learned in these seven chapters. It's the rhythm that keeps the frequency locked in. It's the liturgy that replaces the old Death Ritual with the new Life Liturgy.

For the next thirty days, you will practice what it means to live as a cleansed portal. To walk in the authority of the New Creation. To maintain the Dabeq frequency with the Seventh Man. To guard the doorway of your soul. To testify to what the Blood has done.

This is not a theory anymore. This is not just about understanding the mechanics. This is living the restoration. This is walking in the wholeness. This is becoming the testimony.

The Seventh Man is waiting at the altar. The workbook is the daily meeting place. The restoration is ready to be lived.

It's time to step across the threshold.

Let's begin.

Conclusion: You Are Not Going Back

You are standing at a threshold you've never crossed before. Behind you is the old life, the one where you were defined by your history, enslaved by the cycle, vibrating at the frequency of the Five Husbands. The life where shame whispered your name in the mirror. Where the "55s" played on repeat in your subconscious. Where you carried the weight of generational habits you didn't even know you inherited. That life is over.

Not because you "tried harder." Not because you "got your act together." Not because you finally mustered enough willpower to white-knuckle your way through temptation.

That life is over because the Seventh Man met you at the well. Because the Blood sanctified the portal. Because you renounced the Five, walked through the Wilderness, and cleaved, “Dabeq”, to the One who told you all things that ever you did and loved you anyway. You are not the same person who started reading this book. You are a New Creation. And New Creations don't go back.

The Journey You've Walked

Let's trace the path you've traveled through these seven

chapters. Because understanding where you've been is essential to recognizing where you're going.

You started with The Con. You learned that the "55s", the sexual lies and ideologies embedded in modern media, music, movies, and culture, were not random. They were strategic. Intentional. Designed to groom your soul for bondage. You learned that the enemy doesn't just tempt you with sin; he programs you to crave it. He plants the frequency in your subconscious long before you ever act it out.

And you learned that the con is gendered. Men are groomed to see women as conquests, trophies, objects to be consumed. Women are groomed to see their bodies as currency, their beauty as power, and their sexuality as the only thing that makes them valuable. The "55s" are everywhere, and they've been playing in your mind since childhood. But now you know. The con is exposed. The frequency is identified. And you can't unhear the truth.

Then you learned The Mechanics. You discovered that your soul is not just a vague spiritual concept; it has structure. The Asa (your physical body) and the Bara (your spiritual essence) are designed to function in harmony. You learned that sex is not just a physical act or an emotional connection; it's a blood covenant. A portal. A spiritual welding that fuses two souls into one.

You learned that every sexual encounter, whether in marriage or outside of it, opens a doorway. And when that doorway is opened outside of covenant, it doesn't just affect you. It affects your ancestors. Your descendants. Your entire lineage. You learned that the Cumulative Covenant Effect is real, that the Five Husbands you've been with are still occupying space in your soul, and the Current One cannot heal what the Five broke.

But you also learned that there is hope. Because the mechanics that bind you are the same mechanics that can free you. When you understand how the portal works, you can close it. When you understand the covenant, you can renounce it.

Then came The Diagnosis. You met the Woman at the Well. You saw yourself in her story, the shame, the thirst, the endless search for something to fill the void. You learned that the Five Husbands represent every unholy covenant you've ever entered, every portal you've ever opened, every frequency you've ever vibrated at that wasn't aligned with God's design.

And you learned that the Current One, no matter how good, how loving, how committed, cannot heal the weight of the

Five. Only the Seventh Man can do that. Only Jesus, the One who knows your history and loves you anyway, the One who offers living water that satisfies forever, can break the Cumulative Covenant Effect and set you free.

You learned the pathway to healing: Accept the diagnosis. Acknowledge the Five. Allow the Seventh Man in. And you took the first step toward freedom.

Then you learned The Art of Leaving. You discovered that healing requires severance. You cannot cleave to the Seventh Man while still tethered to the Five. You cannot walk into the new covenant while still honoring the old one. So, you learned to divorce the cultural parents who raised you, the Mother of Shame, the Father of Lust, the Ancestral Altar.

You walked through the Wilderness, the uncomfortable, silent, in-between space where the old is gone but the new hasn't fully arrived. You learned that the Wilderness is not punishment; it's preparation. It's where God rewires your soul, resets your frequency, and teaches you to hear His voice instead of the "55s."

And you issued the Spiritual Bill of Divorcement. You renounced the Five. You returned the property they stole. You changed your name. You severed the ties that bound your soul.

Then you learned The Power of Cleaving. You discovered that cleaving is not codependency. It's not neediness. It's not two broken people clinging to each other for survival. Cleaving is Dabeq, the divine spiritual fusion that God designed from the beginning. It's the holy welding of two whole souls into one unstoppable force.

You learned the three seasons of cleaving: the Courtship of Self (becoming whole alone), the Courtship of Frequency (discerning alignment with another), and the Sealed Covenant (marriage = the ultimate fusion). You learned that the frequency you establish in your marriage doesn't just affect you and your spouse. It opens a generational portal. Your children will inherit the frequency you create.

And you learned that the Seventh Man is the Third Cord in every covenant marriage. He is the One who sustains the fusion, guards the portal, and keeps the frequency locked in.

Then you learned The Ritual of the Soul. You discovered that most people fight the wrong battle at the wrong stage. They try to resist Acting Out when the real battle is in the Fantasy. You learned the anatomy of the cycle: The Lie → The Groove → The Yielding → Acting Out. And you learned that the only way to break the cycle is to interrupt it at the root, in the mind, before the spirit arrives.

You learned to replace Death Rituals with Life Liturgies. To starve the ritual by closing the door before the enemy knocks. To cast down imaginations and replace the "55s" with the "7." To reclaim authority over your own soul, not through white-knuckle discipline, but through legitimate dominion.

And finally, you learned The Altar of Restoration. You discovered that your healing doesn't end with you. Your cleansed portal becomes a weapon. Your testimony becomes evidence. Your scars become credentials. You learned that you are not "recovering", you are restored. You are not a victim; you are a New Creation. You are not broken, you are whole. And you learned that your wholeness flows backward through your ancestral line and forward to your descendants. You are not just breaking the cycle for yourself. You are breaking it for everyone connected to you: past, present, and future.

You are a generational healer. A portal of blessing. A carrier of the Seventh Man's frequency.

The Before and the After

Let's be clear about what has happened.

Before, you were a victim. You were defined by what was done to you, what you did to yourself, and what you inherited from those who came before you. You were enslaved by the cycle. Bound by the Five. Vibrating at the frequency of shame, lust, rejection, trauma, and generational habits.

You were a curse carrier. Every unholy covenant you entered opened a portal that flowed downward to your children and upward to your ancestors. You were passing on the same bondage you inherited. The same lies. The same cycles. The same frequency.

After, you are a New Creation. You are defined by the Blood of the Lamb, not the blood of your past. You are free from the cycle. Divorced from the Five. Cleaved to the Seventh Man. Vibrating at the frequency of heaven.

You are a blessing carrier. Every portal you've closed, every covenant you've renounced, every frequency you've shifted, it all flows backward and forward through your lineage. You are healing your ancestors. You are blessing your descendants. You are establishing a new pattern, a new rhythm, a new legacy. This is not hyperbole. This is not motivational fluff. This is a spiritual reality. When God looks at you now, He doesn't see the Five Husbands. He doesn't see your history. He doesn't see the shame, the trauma, the cycles, the failures.

He sees Blood. He sees the Seventh Man standing in the doorway of your soul, guarding the portal, declaring over you:

"This one is Mine. This one is clean. This one is whole. This one is a New Creation." And if that's how God sees you, that's how you must see yourself.

The Generational and Kingdom Impact

But here's what you need to understand: your healing is not just about you. This is bigger than your personal freedom. This is bigger than your marriage. This is bigger than your family. Your wholeness is a threat to the enemy's kingdom.

Because when you walk in freedom, when you testify to what the Blood has done, when you live as a cleansed portal, when you vibrate at the frequency of the Seventh Man, you become inexplicable evidence that God is real. That healing is possible. That the cycle can be broken. And that provokes the city.

The Woman at the Well didn't just get healed and go home. She left her waterpot at the well and walked into the city in broad daylight. She testified to the very men who knew her history. She said, "Come and see a man who told me all things that ever I did. Is not this the Christ?" And the city was shaken. Many believed because of her testimony.

This is what happens when you stop hiding and start testifying. This is what happens when you walk in the authority of the New Creation. This is what happens when you become a portal of blessing instead of a portal of bondage.

Your freedom exposes the "55s" as the lie they always were. Your wholeness proves that the enemy's system of sexual enslavement is not unbreakable. Your testimony becomes weaponized evidence in the courts of heaven. And your children, your children will walk in a different frequency than the one you inherited. They will not carry the shame you carried. They will not fight the battles you fought. They will not vibrate at the frequency of the Five Husbands.

They will inherit the frequency of the Seventh Man. Because you broke the cycle. Because you purged the portal. Because you established a new pattern. This is generational healing. This is Kingdom advancement. This is spiritual warfare at the highest level.

The Authority You Now Possess

Let's talk about the authority you're walking into.

You are not a victim anymore. You are not enslaved anymore. You are not at the mercy of the cycle, the Five, the "55s," or the enemy's lies. You have authority over your own soul now.

You decide which portals stay open and which stay closed. You decide which frequencies you vibrate and which you silence. You decide which covenants you honor and which you renounce.

This is not arrogance. This is not pride. This is not you trying to be something you're not. This is the legitimate reclamation of dominion. This is you stepping into the role God designed you for from the beginning: a steward of your own life, a guardian of your own soul, a gatekeeper of your own spirit.

And when you walk in that authority, when you declare, "This portal is closed. This frequency is locked in. This cycle is broken. This covenant is sealed", the enemy has no choice but to obey.

Because you're not speaking from your own power. You're speaking from the authority of the Blood. You're declaring the truth of the New Creation. You're standing in the identity of the sanctified portal. And that authority is unshakable. Unbreakable. Unstoppable. This is who you are now. This is the power you're walking in. This is the freedom you've been given.

Don't shrink back from it. Don't apologize for it. Don't let shame or fear or the enemy's lies convince you that you're not worthy of it. You are a New Creation. You are a cleansed portal. You are a generational healer. You are a carrier of the Seventh Man's frequency.

Walk in it. Declare it. Live it.

The Workbook: Stewardship, Not Punishment

The Workbook: Stewardship, Not Punishment

Now, let's talk about the next thirty days.

The 30-Day Workbook that follows is not "more work." It's not a list of religious obligations. It's not punishment for past failures. It's not a test to see if you're "serious enough" about your healing.

The workbook is stewardship. It's the daily maintenance of the altar you've built. It's the practical, tangible, lived-out expression of everything you've learned in these seven chapters.

Think of it this way: you've been given a gift. The Seventh Man has healed your soul, cleansed your portal, shifted your frequency, and sealed your covenant. But a gift that's not stewarded is a gift that's wasted. The workbook is how you steward the healing. It's how you maintain the frequency. It's how you guard the portal. It's how you replace the old Death Rituals with the new Life Liturgies.

For the next thirty days, you will practice what it means to live as a New Creation. To walk in the authority of the cleansed portal. To maintain the Dabeq frequency with the Seventh

Man. To testify to what the Blood has done.

This is not theory anymore. This is not just about understanding the mechanics. This is living the restoration. This is walking in the wholeness. This is becoming the testimony.

And here's the beautiful part: the Seventh Man meets you in the daily liturgy. Every morning when you open the workbook, He's there. Every time you pray the prayers, declare the truths, practice the rhythms, He's there. Sustaining you. Strengthening you. Sealing the covenant deeper and deeper into your soul. This is not a grind. This is not bondage. This is the rhythm of freedom.

You Are Not Going Back

So here's the declaration I want you to make—out loud, with authority, with conviction:

I am not going back.

I am not going back to the cycle. I am not going back to the Five. I am not going back to the frequency of shame, lust, rejection, trauma, or generational habits.

I am not going back to the "55s." I am not going back to the lie that my body is currency, that my sexuality is power, that my worth is determined by who wants me.

I am not going back to the Death Ritual. I am not going back to the fantasy, the groove, the yielding, the acting out. I am not going back to the portal that was opened to hell.

I am a New Creation. Old things have passed away. All things have become new. I am a cleansed portal. I am a generational healer. I am a carrier of the Seventh Man's frequency. I am a testimony-bearer. I am a weapon in the hands of God.

I have authority over my own soul. I decide which portals stay open. I decide which frequencies I vibrate at. I decide which covenants I honor. And I have decided: I am cleaved "Dabeq" to the Seventh Man. I am sealed in the covenant. I am walking in the authority of the Blood.

I am not going back.

The city is waiting for your testimony. Your children are waiting to inherit a different frequency. The Seventh Man is waiting at the altar. The next thirty days will prove that healing is not a theory. It's a lived reality. It's a daily practice. It's a rhythm of freedom.

You are not going back. You are stepping forward.

Let's begin.

THE 30-DAY SACRED SYNERGY WORKBOOK

A Daily Guide to Fusing Souls and Breaking Cycles

Introduction:

This workbook is your daily "altar." For the next thirty days, you and your spouse (or you as an individual preparing for covenant) will engage in the spiritual and physical work of Dabeq—the holy welding of two into one. We are moving beyond the "55" cultural delusions and into the "Seventh Man" restoration.

How to Use This Workbook

This is not a checklist. This is not a religious obligation. This is not punishment for past failures.

This is stewardship. This is the daily maintenance of the altar you've built. This is the practical, tangible, lived-out expression of everything you've learned in the previous seven chapters.

For the next thirty days, you will practice what it means to live as a New Creation. To walk in the authority of the cleansed portal. To maintain the Dabeq frequency with the Seventh Man. To testify to what the Blood has done.

Each day includes:

- Today's Focus: The specific work you're doing today
- The Practice: Concrete, actionable steps
- Your Frequency Work: How to recognize and shift your spiritual vibration
- The Liturgy: A short declaration or prayer to replace old death rituals
- Authority Declaration: A statement you speak aloud to reclaim dominion
- Journaling Prompt: Deep reflection questions
- Closing Prayer: A 30-second to 1-minute prayer sealing the day's work

A few guidelines:

Do this work in the morning if possible. Set the frequency for your day.

Speak the declarations OUT LOUD. Your voice has authority.

Don't rush. If a day requires more time, take it.

If you're married, do this work together when possible. If you're single, do it in preparation for covenant.

Keep a journal nearby. Write what the Spirit reveals.

The Seventh Man meets you here. Every single day.

WEEK 1: THE INVENTORY (Days 1-7)

Theme: Identifying What Needs to Be Healed

Day 1: The Inventory of the Five

Today's Focus: You cannot heal what you will not name. Today, you take inventory of every unholy covenant you've entered, every sexual relationship, every emotional entanglement, every portal you've opened outside of God's design.

The Practice:

In your journal, write the heading: "The Five Husbands."

List every person you've been sexually intimate with (including emotional affairs, pornography "relationships," or fantasy bonds that felt like covenant).

For each one, write one sentence: "I opened a portal with [name/description]. I acknowledge the covenant I entered."

Do not shame yourself. Do not justify. Simply name it.

When you're finished, read the list aloud to the Seventh Man. Say: "Jesus, I bring these Five to You. I cannot heal this alone. Only You can close what I opened."

<u>Your Frequency Work</u>: Notice the weight in your chest as you

write. That heaviness is the Cumulative Covenant Effect, the spiritual reality of multiple covenants occupying the same soul. You're not imagining it. It's real. Acknowledge it: "I feel the weight of the Five. I am ready to be free."

The Liturgy (Speak aloud): "I acknowledge the Five. I bring them to the Seventh Man. I cannot heal this alone, but He can. I am not defined by my history. I am defined by the Blood."

Authority Declaration: "I have authority to name what needs healing. I am not hiding anymore."

Journaling Prompt:

Which of the Five still occupies the most space in your soul? Why?

What would it feel like to be completely free of their influence?

Closing Prayer: "Heavenly Father, I have named the Five. I have brought them into the light. I ask You to begin the work of closing every portal I opened. I trust You to heal what I cannot heal. I am Yours, In Jesus' Name. Amen."

Day 2: Mapping the Shame

Today's Focus: Shame is not just an emotion; it's a voice. Today, you identify where the mother of shame planted her lies in your soul. You map the terrain of your shame so you can begin to evict her.

The Practice:

In your journal, write the heading: "The Voice of Shame."

Write down every shameful message you've internalized about your body, your sexuality, your worth. Examples:

"You're damaged goods."

"No one will want you if they knew."

"You're too much / not enough."

"Your body is the problem."

For each lie, identify where it came from: a parent, a partner, the church, the culture, or a traumatic experience.

Read the list aloud. Then say: "These are lies. The Mother of Shame planted these. I reject them."

<u>Your Frequency Work</u>: Shame vibrates at a low, suffocating frequency. As you read the lies aloud, notice the tightness in your throat, the heat in your face, the urge to hide. That's the frequency of shame. Now take a deep breath and say: "I am not ashamed. I am loved." Feel the shift—even if it's small.

The Liturgy (Speak aloud): "The Mother of Shame does not define me. Her voice is not my voice. I am not damaged. I am not too much. I am not too little. I am loved by the Seventh

Man, and that is enough."

Authority Declaration: "I have the authority to silence the voice of shame. I decide what I believe about myself."

Journaling Prompt:

When did you first hear the voice of shame? What was the moment?

What would your life look like if shame had no voice in your soul?

Closing Prayer: "Father, in the name of Jesus, I reject the lies of the mother of shame. I silence her voice. I choose to believe what You say about me: I am loved, I am whole, I am Yours. Amen."

Day 3: The "55s" You've Absorbed

Today's Focus: The "55s"—the sexual lies and ideologies embedded in modern culture—have been playing in your subconscious for years. Today, you identify which "55s" you've absorbed and begin to replace them with the "7" (God's truth).

The Practice:

In your journal, write the heading: "The '55s' I've Believed."

List the cultural lies you've internalized about sex, bodies, pleasure, masculinity, or femininity. Examples:

"Sex is just physical."

"My body is my power."

"Real men conquer."

"I have to perform to be loved."

"Pleasure is the goal."

For each "55," write the "7" (the truth) next to it. Example:

"55": "Sex is just physical." → "7": "Sex is a blood covenant that opens spiritual portals."

Read the "7s" aloud. Let the truth replace the lie.

Your Frequency Work: The "55s" create a chaotic, dissonant frequency in your soul. As you read the lies, notice the confusion, the pull, the familiarity. Now read the "7s" aloud and notice the clarity, the peace, the alignment. That's the frequency of truth.

The Liturgy (Speak aloud): "I reject the '55s' the world has planted in my mind. I choose the '7'—the truth of God's design. My body is not currency. My sexuality is not power. I am a covenant-keeper, not a consumer."

Authority Declaration: "I have authority to reject the '55s' and choose the '7.' I decide what plays in my mind."

Journaling Prompt:

Which "55" has been the hardest to let go of? Why?

What would it feel like to live fully in the "7"?

Closing Prayer:" Father, in the matchless name of Jesus, I reject the '55s.' I choose the ‘7’ man, Jesus Christ. Rewire my mind. Reset my frequency. Teach me to see sex, bodies, and covenant the way You do. Amen."

Day 4: The Lust Frequency

Today's Focus: Lust is not just temptation; it's a frequency. The Father of Lust has been modeling a pattern of consumption, control, and conquest. Today, you identify how lust was planted in your soul and begin to starve it.

The Practice:

In your journal, write the heading: "The Father of Lust."

Answer these questions:

How was lust modeled in your home growing up? (A parent's affair, pornography, objectification, control?)

What did you learn about sex from the men (or women) in your life?

When did you first feel the pull of lust? What was the context?

Write one sentence: "The Father of Lust taught me that [fill in the blank]. I reject this pattern."

Declare aloud: "I am not my father. I am not my mother. I am a New Creation."

Your Frequency Work: Lust vibrates at a frantic, consuming, frequently hungry, never satisfied. Notice where you feel it in your body: the restlessness, the craving, the urgency. Now breathe deeply and say: "I am not controlled by lust. I am led by the Spirit." Feel the frequency shift from frantic to steady.

The Liturgy (Speak aloud): "The Father of Lust does not control me. I am not a consumer. I am not a conqueror. I am a covenant-keeper. I reject the frequency of lust and choose the frequency of love."

Authority Declaration: "I have authority over the lust frequency. I starve what I do not feed."

Journaling Prompt:

What does lust promise you? What does it actually deliver?

What would it feel like to be completely free of lust's pulling?

Closing Prayer: "Jesus, I reject the Father of Lust. I renounce the pattern of consumption and control. Teach me to love, not lust. Teach me to honor, not objectify. I am Yours. Amen."

Day 5: The Generational Backpack

Today's Focus: You are carrying a backpack full of generational patterns, survival lies, and ancestral wounds. Today, you identify what you've inherited and begin to set it down.

The Practice:

In your journal, write the heading: "The Generational Backpack."

List the patterns you've inherited from your family line:

Sexual dysfunction (affairs, abuse, addiction)

Relational patterns (divorce, abandonment, control)

Survival lies ("Don't trust anyone," "Sex is power," "Men/women can't be trusted")

For each pattern, write: "I inherited [pattern], but I am breaking the cycle."

Declare aloud: "I am not bound by my ancestors' choices. I am a generational healer."

<u>Your Frequency Work</u>: Generational patterns vibrate at a heavy, familiar frequency, like a weight you've carried so long you forgot it was there. As you name the patterns, notice the heaviness in your shoulders and your chest. Now say: "I set

down the backpack. I am not carrying this anymore." Feel the lightness begin.

The Liturgy (Speak aloud): "I am not bound by my ancestors' choices. I am not carrying their shame, their dysfunction, their survival lies. I am a generational healer. I break the cycle here."

Authority Declaration: "I have the authority to set down what I did not choose to carry. I am free."

Journaling Prompt:

What pattern are you most afraid of repeating?

What would it mean for your children if you broke this cycle?

Closing Prayer: "Father, I set down the generational backpack. I am not carrying my ancestors' wounds anymore. I am a healer, not a curse-carrier. Break the cycle in me. Amen."

Day 6: The Weight of the Five

Today's Focus: The Cumulative Covenant Effect is real. Today, you acknowledge the spiritual weight of the Five Husbands and prepare to release it to the Seventh Man.

The Practice:

In your journal, write the heading: "The Weight of the Five."

Describe the weight you feel: Is it in your chest? Your shoulders? Your mind? Your body?

Write one sentence for each of the Five: "I feel the weight of [name/description]. I am ready to release it."

Pray aloud: "Jesus, I cannot carry this weight anymore. I give You the Five. Take the weight. Close the portals. Set me free."

Your Frequency Work: The weight of the Five creates a dense, suffocating frequency. As you acknowledge it, notice the pressure, the exhaustion, the sense of being trapped. Now imagine the Seventh Man standing in front of you, reaching out His hand. Say: "I give You the weight." Feel the release—even if it's just a breath.

The Liturgy (Speak aloud):"I acknowledge the weight of the Five. I cannot carry it anymore. I give it to the Seventh Man. He is strong enough to carry what I cannot."

Authority Declaration: "I have authority to release what I cannot carry. I am not alone."

Journaling Prompt:

What would it feel like to wake up without this weight?

What are you afraid will happen if you let it go?

Closing Prayer:" Jesus, I give You the weight of the Five. I cannot carry it anymore. Take it. Close the portals. Set me free. I trust You. Amen."

Day 7: Diagnostic Moment—The Truth You're Ready to Admit

Today's Focus: This is your diagnostic moment. Today, you admit the truth you've been avoiding: what needs to change, what needs to be healed, what needs to be severed. This is the moment the Woman at the Well said, "I have no husband."

The Practice:

In your journal, write the heading: "The Truth I'm Ready to Admit."

Complete this sentence: "The truth is, I need healing in [specific area]."

Be specific. Don't generalize. Examples:

"The truth is, I am still bound to my ex."

"The truth is, I am addicted to pornography."

"The truth is, I am afraid of intimacy."

"The truth is, I don't know how to be loved without performing."

Read it aloud to the Seventh Man. Say: "This is the truth. I am ready to be healed."

Your Frequency Work: Truth vibrates at a clear, piercing frequency. As you speak the truth aloud, notice the clarity, the relief, the fear. That's the frequency of honesty. Now say: "I am not hiding anymore. I am ready to be free." Feel the shift from hiding to openness.

The Liturgy (Speak aloud):"I admit the truth. I am not hiding anymore. I am ready to be healed. The Seventh Man knows my history and loves me anyway. I am safe to be honest."

Authority Declaration:"I have authority to speak the truth about my own life. I am not hiding anymore."

Journaling Prompt:

What has it cost you to hide the truth?

What will it cost you to keep hiding?

Closing Prayer: "Jesus, I have spoken the truth. I am not hiding anymore. I am ready to be healed. Meet me here. I trust You. Amen."

WEEK 2: THE LIBERATION (Days 8-14)

Theme: Breaking Free from Unholy Ties

Day 8: The Renouncement Begins

Today's Focus: Today, you issue your first Spiritual Bill of Divorcement. You formally renounce the Mother of Shame and sever her authority over your soul.

The Practice:

In your journal, write the heading: "Spiritual Bill of Divorcement: The Mother of Shame."

Write this declaration:

"I, [your name], formally renounce the Mother of Shame. I divorce her voice from my soul. I return every lie she planted. I reclaim my identity as beloved, whole, and free. She has no authority over me. I am a New Creation."

Read it aloud with conviction.

Tear the page out of your journal (or mark it with a line) as a symbolic act of severance.

Your Frequency Work: Renouncement creates a sharp, decisive frequency, like cutting a cord. As you speak the words, notice the clarity, the finality, the authority in your voice. That's the frequency of freedom. Say: "I am free from shame. I am beloved." Feel the shift.

The Liturgy (Speak aloud):"I renounce the Mother of Shame. I divorce her voice. I am not ashamed. I am beloved. I am whole. I am free."

Authority Declaration: "I have authority to divorce what was never mine to carry. I am free."

Journaling Prompt:

What does it feel like to formally renounce shame?

What would your life look like if shame had no voice?

Closing Prayer: "Jesus, I have renounced the Mother of Shame. I am free from her voice. I am beloved. I am whole. I am Yours. Amen."

Day 9: Returning the Property

Today's Focus: Every unholy covenant you entered gave the other person (or spirit) access to your soul. Today, you return the property they stole: your peace, your identity, your authority, your joy.

The Practice:

In your journal, write the heading: "Returning the Property."

For each of the Five (or the Mother of Shame, Father of Lust, etc.), write what they took from you. Examples:

"You took my peace."

"You took my sense of safety."

"You took my joy."

"You took my identity."

For each one, write: "I take back [what was stolen]. It is mine. You have no claim to it."

Declare aloud: "I return what you gave me (shame, lies, control), and I take back what you stole. I am whole."

Your Frequency Work: Returning property creates a reclaiming frequency, strong, clear, authoritative. As you speak, notice the strength in your voice, the clarity in your mind. That's the frequency of authority. Say: "I take back what is mine. I am whole." Feel the shift.

The Liturgy (Speak aloud):"I return what you gave me. I take back what you stole. My peace is mine. My joy is mine. My identity is mine. You have no claim to me."

Authority Declaration: "I have authority to reclaim what was stolen. I am whole."

Journaling Prompt:

What was the most valuable thing stolen from you?

What does it feel like to take it back?

Closing Prayer: "Jesus, I take back what was stolen. I return what was never mine. I am whole. I am free. I am Yours. Amen."

Day 10: Changing Your Name From Shame

Today's Focus: In the Bible, a name change signifies a new identity. Today, you change your name from what shame called you to what the Seventh Man calls you.

The Practice:

In your journal, write the heading: "My Old Name vs. My New Name."

In the left column, write what shame called you: "Damaged," "Unworthy," "Too Much," "Not Enough," etc.

In the right column, write what the Seventh Man calls you: "Beloved," "Whole," "Redeemed," "New Creation," "Mine."

Cross out the old names. Circle the new names.

Declare aloud: "My name is no longer [old name]. My name is [new name]. I am who the Seventh Man says I am."

Your Frequency Work: A name change creates a transformative frequency, like stepping into a new identity. As you speak your new name, notice the shift in your posture, your breath, your sense of self. That's the frequency of the New Creation. Say: "I am [new name]. I am beloved." Feel the shift.

The Liturgy (Speak aloud):"My name is no longer Shame. My name is Beloved. My name is no longer Broken. My name is Whole. I am who the Seventh Man says I am."

Authority Declaration: "I have authority to change my name. I am a New Creation."

Journaling Prompt:

What does it feel like to be called by your new name?

How would you live differently if you believed your new name?

Closing Prayer: "Jesus, I receive my new name. I am Beloved. I am Whole. I am Yours. Thank You for calling me by name. Amen."

Day 11: The Father of Lust Severance

Today's Focus: Today, you issue your second Spiritual Bill of Divorcement. You formally renounce the Father of Lust and sever his authority over your sexuality.

The Practice:

In your journal, write the heading: "Spiritual Bill of

Divorcement: The Father of Lust."

Write this declaration:

"I, [your name], formally renounce the Father of Lust. I divorce his pattern of consumption, control, and conquest from my soul. I return every lie he planted. I reclaim my sexuality as sacred, covenant, and holy. He has no authority over me. I am a New Creation."

Read it aloud with conviction.

Tear the page out or mark it as a symbolic act of severance.

Your Frequency Work: Renouncing lust creates a purifying frequency, like fire burning away impurity. As you speak, notice the clarity, the strength, the authority. That's the frequency of holiness. Say: "I am not controlled by lust. I am led by love." Feel the shift.

The Liturgy (Speak aloud):"I renounce the Father of Lust. I divorce his pattern. I am not a consumer. I am a covenant-keeper. I am holy. I am free."

Authority Declaration: "I have authority over my sexuality. I am not controlled by lust."

Journaling Prompt:

What does it feel like to renounce lust?

What would your sexuality look like if it were fully redeemed?

Closing Prayer: "Jesus, I have renounced the Father of Lust. I am free from his pattern. I am holy. I am Yours. Amen."

Day 12: Returning the Inheritance of Lies

Today's Focus: Today, you return the generational inheritance of lies, dysfunction, and survival patterns. You break the ancestral altar and establish a new pattern.

The Practice:

In your journal, write the heading: "Returning the Inheritance."

List the generational patterns you identified on Day 5.

For each one, write: "I return [pattern] to the generation that created it. I do not carry this anymore. I break the cycle here."

Declare aloud: "I am not bound by my ancestors' choices. I am a generational healer. I establish a new pattern."

Your Frequency Work: Breaking generational patterns creates a liberating frequency, like chains falling off. As you speak, notice the lightness, the freedom, the authority. That's the frequency of generational healing. Say: "I break the cycle. I am free." Feel the shift.

The Liturgy (Speak aloud):"I return the inheritance of lies. I break the ancestral altar. I am not bound by my ancestors' choices. I am a generational healer. I establish a new pattern."

Authority Declaration: "I have the authority to break generational cycles. I am a healer, not a curse-carrier."

Journaling Prompt:

What new pattern are you establishing for your descendants?

What will your children inherit from you?

Closing Prayer: "Jesus, I return the inheritance of lies. I break the cycle. I am a generational healer. Establish a new pattern in me. Amen."

Day 13: The Wilderness Walk

Today's Focus: The Wilderness is the in-between space—the uncomfortable, silent season where the old is gone but the new hasn't fully arrived. Today, you embrace the Wilderness as preparation, not punishment.

The Practice:

In your journal, write the heading: "The Wilderness."

Describe where you are right now: What feels uncomfortable? What feels uncertain? What feels silent?

Write this declaration: "The Wilderness is not punishment. It is preparation. God is rewiring my soul, resetting my frequency, teaching me to hear His voice."

Sit in silence for 5 minutes. Don't fill the space. Just listen.

Your Frequency Work: The Wilderness vibrates at a quiet, steady frequency, like a hum beneath the noise. As you sit in silence, notice the discomfort, the urge to fill the space. Resist it. Say: "I am safe in the Wilderness. God is with me." Feel the shift from anxiety to peace.

The Liturgy (Speak aloud): "The Wilderness is not punishment. It is preparation. I am safe here. God is rewiring my soul. I am learning to hear His voice."

Authority Declaration: "I have authority to embrace the Wilderness. I am not afraid of the silence."

Journaling Prompt:

What is God teaching you in the Wilderness?
What are you afraid will happen if you stay here?

Closing Prayer: "Jesus, I embrace the Wilderness. I am not afraid. You are with me. Teach me to hear Your voice. Amen."

Day 14: The Frequency of Freedom

Today's Focus: Today, you experience the frequency of freedom for the first time. You are no longer bound by the Five, the shame, the lust, the generational patterns. You are free. And freedom has a frequency.

The Practice:

In your journal, write the heading: "The Frequency of Freedom."

Describe what freedom feels like in your body: Is it light? Spacious? Peaceful? Strong?

Write this declaration: "I am free. I am no longer bound by my history. I am a New Creation. I vibrate at the frequency of freedom."

Stand up. Take a deep breath. Say aloud: "I am free." Feel it in your body.

Your Frequency Work: Freedom vibrates at a light, expansive frequency—like wings unfolding. As you speak, notice the lightness in your chest, the clarity in your mind, the strength in your voice. That's the frequency of freedom. Say: "I am free. I am whole. I am loved." Feel the shift.

The Liturgy (Speak aloud): "I am free. I am no longer bound by my history. I am a New Creation. I vibrate at the frequency of freedom. I am whole. I am loved. I am His."

Authority Declaration: "I have authority to walk in freedom. I am not going back."

Journaling Prompt:

What does freedom feel like?

What will you do with your freedom?

Closing Prayer: "Jesus, I am free. Thank You for breaking the chains. Thank You for setting me free. I am Yours. Amen."

WEEK 3: THE RESTORATION (Days 15-21)

Theme: Breaking the Cycle and Establishing New Rhythms

Day 15: Mapping Your Trigger

Today's Focus: Every cycle has a trigger—a specific event, emotion, or circumstance that activates the fantasy. Today, you map your trigger so you can interrupt the cycle at the root.

The Practice:

In your journal, write the heading: "My Trigger."

Answer these questions:

What emotion usually precedes the fantasy? (Loneliness, stress, boredom, rejection, anger?)

What circumstance activates it? (Being alone, late at night, after conflict, after success?)

What does the trigger promise you? (Comfort, escape, control, validation?)

Write one sentence: "My trigger is [emotion/circumstance]. It promises [false promise]. I recognize it now."

Declare aloud: "I see the trigger. I will not be ambushed anymore."

Your Frequency Work: Triggers vibrate at a chaotic, urgent frequency, like an alarm going off. As you identify your trigger, notice the activation in your body: the restlessness, the craving, the urgency. Now say: "I see the trigger. I am not controlled by it." Feel the shift from reactive to aware.

The Liturgy (Speak aloud):"I see my trigger. I recognize the lie it tells. I am not controlled by it. I am aware. I am awake. I am free."

Authority Declaration: "I have authority to recognize my trigger. I will not be ambushed."

Journaling Prompt:

What does your trigger promise you?

What does it actually deliver?

Closing Prayer: "Jesus, I see my trigger. I am not controlled by it. Give me awareness. Give me strength. I am Yours. Amen."

Day 16: Interrupting the Fantasy

Today's Focus: The battle is won or lost in the mind. Today, you practice 2 Corinthians 10:5—casting down imaginations and replacing the "55s" with the "7."

The Practice:

In your journal, write the heading: "Interrupting the Fantasy."

Identify the specific fantasy that usually follows your trigger. Don't shame yourself, just name it.

Write the "55" (the lie the fantasy tells): "This will satisfy you. This will make you feel powerful. This will fill the void."

Write the "7" (the truth): "This is a lie. This will leave you empty. Only the Seventh Man can satisfy."

Practice this out loud: When the fantasy begins, say immediately: "This is a lie. I cast it down. I choose the truth."

Your Frequency Work: Fantasy vibrates at a seductive, hypnotic frequency, like a siren song. As you practice interrupting it, notice the resistance, the pull, the discomfort. That's the frequency of warfare. Now say: "I cast down this imagination. I choose the truth." Feel the shift from seduction to clarity.

The Liturgy (Speak aloud):"I cast down imaginations. I take every thought captive. I replace the '55' with the '7.' I choose truth. I choose freedom. I choose the Seventh Man."

Authority Declaration: "I have authority over my own mind. I decide what I think about."

Journaling Prompt:

What does the fantasy promise you?

What truth do you need to replace it with?

Closing Prayer: "Jesus, I cast down imaginations. I take every thought captive. Give me the strength to choose truth. I am Yours. Amen."

Day 17: Identifying Your Ritual

Today's Focus: The ritual is the series of grooming behaviors that lead to Acting Out. Today, you identify your specific ritual so you can starve it before it gains momentum.

The Practice:

In your journal, write the heading: "My Ritual."

Map the steps of your ritual. Be specific. Examples:

"I isolate myself."

"I scroll social media late at night."

"I pick a fight with my spouse."

"I tell myself I deserve this."

"I open the app / website / drawer."

For each step, write: "This is part of the ritual. I am closing this door."

Declare aloud: "I see the ritual. I will not participate in it anymore."

Your Frequency Work: The ritual vibrates at a familiar, automatic frequency, like muscle memory. As you identify the steps, notice the pull, the familiarity, the sense of inevitability. That's the frequency of the ritual. Now say: "I see the ritual. I am not controlled by it." Feel the shift from automatic to intentional.

The Liturgy (Speak aloud): "I see my ritual. I recognize the steps. I am not controlled by it. I close the door before the spirit arrives. I am free."

Authority Declaration: "I have authority to starve the ritual. I close the door."

Journaling Prompt:

What is the first step of your ritual?

What would happen if you interrupted it there?

Closing Prayer: "Jesus, I see my ritual. I am not controlled by it. Give me the strength to close the door. I am Yours. Amen."

Day 18: Starving the Ritual

Today's Focus: Today, you create practical barriers to starve the ritual. You remove access, create accountability, and build friction before the cycle gains momentum.

The Practice:

In your journal, write the heading: "Starving the Ritual."

For each step of your ritual (from Day 17), write one practical barrier. Examples:

"I will not be alone late at night." (Barrier: Go to bed at the same time as my spouse.)

"I will not scroll social media after 9 PM." (Barrier: Put my phone in another room.)

"I will not isolate when I'm triggered." (Barrier: Call a friend / pray / go for a walk.)

Implement one barrier today. Just one.

Declare aloud: "I am starving the ritual. I am creating friction. I am free."

Your Frequency Work: Starving the ritual creates a disruptive frequency, like throwing sand in the gears. As you implement barriers, notice the resistance, the discomfort, the urge to give up. That's the frequency of change. Say: "I am starving the ritual. I am free." Feel the shift from automatic to intentional.

The Liturgy (Speak aloud): "I am starving the ritual. I am

creating friction. I am removing access. I am closing the door before the spirit arrives. I am free."

Authority Declaration: "I have authority to create barriers. I am not a victim of the cycle."

Journaling Prompt:

What barrier did you implement today?

What did it feel like to disrupt the ritual?

Closing Prayer: "Jesus, I am starving the ritual. Give me the strength to maintain the barriers. I am Yours. Amen."

Day 19: Building Your First Life Liturgy

Today's Focus: Death Rituals must be replaced with Life Liturgies. Today, you create your first Life Liturgy, a specific prayer, practice, or presence you turn to when the trigger hits.

The Practice:

In your journal, write the heading: "My Life Liturgy."

Create a simple, repeatable practice to replace the Death Ritual. Examples:

"When I feel the trigger, I will pray: 'Jesus, I give You this pain. I choose You.'"

"When I feel the trigger, I will call my spouse / friend / accountability partner."

"When I feel the trigger, I will go for a walk and worship."

Write your Life Liturgy in one sentence.

Practice it out loud three times.

Declare aloud: "This is my Life Liturgy. This is what I do when the pain hits."

Your Frequency Work: Life Liturgies vibrate at a grounding, centering frequency, like an anchor in a storm. As you practice your liturgy, notice the calm, the clarity, the sense of being held. That's the frequency of life. Say: "I choose life. I choose the Seventh Man." Feel the shift from chaos to peace.

The Liturgy (Speak aloud): "This is my Life Liturgy. When the pain hits, I turn to the Seventh Man. I do not turn to the ritual. I choose life. I choose freedom. I choose Him."

Authority Declaration: "I have authority to choose life. I am not controlled by the ritual."

Journaling Prompt:

What is your Life Liturgy?

What does it feel like to have a new response to pain?

Closing Prayer: "Jesus, this is my Life Liturgy. When the pain hits, I turn to You. Give me the strength to choose life. I am Yours. Amen."

Day 20: Practicing High-Frequency Warfare

Today's Focus: Spiritual warfare is not passive. Today, you practice speaking truth into the atmosphere, declaring the authority of the Blood, and shifting the frequency of your environment.

The Practice:

In your journal, write the heading: "High-Frequency Warfare."

Write three declarations you will speak aloud when the enemy attacks. Examples:

"I am covered by the Blood of Jesus. The enemy has no authority here."

"I am a New Creation. Old things have passed away."

"I am not going back. I am free."

Stand up. Speak each declaration aloud with authority. Feel the shift in the atmosphere.

Declare aloud: "I am a warrior. I speak truth into the atmosphere. I shift the frequency."

Your Frequency Work: High-frequency warfare vibrates at a powerful, authoritative frequency—like a trumpet blast. As you speak, notice the strength in your voice, the clarity in your mind, the shift in the atmosphere. That's the frequency of authority. Say: "I am a warrior. I speak truth." Feel the shift.

The Liturgy (Speak aloud): "I am a warrior. I speak truth into the atmosphere. I am covered by the Blood. I am a New Creation. I am not going back. I am free."

Authority Declaration: "I have authority to speak truth. I shift the frequency."

Journaling Prompt:

What does it feel like to speak with authority?
What shifts when you declare truth?

Closing Prayer: "Jesus, I am a warrior. I speak truth. I shift the frequency. Give me boldness. I am Yours. Amen."

Day 21: Authority Over Your Own Soul

Today's Focus: Today, you declare the full authority you've reclaimed over your own soul. You are not a victim. You are a steward. You decide which portals stay open, which frequencies you vibrate at, which covenants you honor.

The Practice:

In your journal, write the heading: "Authority Over My Soul."

Write this declaration:

"I, [your name], have authority over my own soul. I decide which portals stay open and which stay closed. I decide which frequencies I vibrate at. I decide which covenants I honor. I am not a victim. I am a steward. I am a New Creation."

Read it aloud with conviction.

Stand up. Place your hand over your heart. Say: "I have authority over my soul. I am free."

Your Frequency Work: Authority vibrates at a steady, unshakable frequency, like a foundation. As you speak, notice the strength, the clarity, the sense of dominion. That's the frequency of authority. Say: "I have authority. I am free." Feel the shift.

The Liturgy (Speak aloud): "I have authority over my own soul. I decide which portals stay open. I decide which frequencies I vibrate at. I am not a victim. I am a steward. I am free."

Authority Declaration: "I have authority over my soul. I am not going back."

Journaling Prompt:

What does it feel like to have authority over your soul?

How will you steward this authority?

Closing Prayer: "Jesus, I have authority over my soul. Thank You for restoring my dominion. I am a steward. I am free. I am

Yours. Amen."

WEEK 4: THE ASCENSION (Days 22-30)

Theme: Walking as New Creation and Establishing Generational Blessing

Day 22: The New Creation Identity

Today's Focus: You are not "recovering." You are not "working on yourself." You are a New Creation. Old things have passed away. All things have become new. Today, you step fully into this identity.

The Practice:

In your journal, write the heading: "I Am a New Creation."

Read 2 Corinthians 5:17 aloud: "Therefore if any man be in Christ, he is a new creature: old things are passed away; behold, all things are become new."

Write this declaration:

"I am not recovering. I am not broken. I am not a victim. I am a New Creation. Old things have passed away. All things have become new. I am whole. I am free. I am His."

Read it aloud three times. Believe it.

Your Frequency Work: The New Creation vibrates at a radiant, transformative frequency—like light breaking through darkness. As you speak, notice the shift in your posture, your breath, your sense of self. That's the frequency of the New Creation. Say: "I am new. I am whole. I am free." Feel the shift.

The Liturgy (Speak aloud):"I am a New Creation. Old things have passed away. All things have become new. I am not recovering. I am transformed. I am whole. I am free. I am His."

Authority Declaration: "I am a New Creation. I am not going back."

Journaling Prompt:

What does it mean to be a New Creation?

How does this identity change the way you see yourself?

Closing Prayer: "Jesus, I am a New Creation. Thank You for making me new. I am whole. I am free. I am Yours. Amen."

Day 23: Your Cleansed Portal

Today's Focus: God has sanctified your history. Your portal is cleansed. Your scars are proof of the Surgeon's skill, not evidence of shame. Today, you receive the cleansed portal.

The Practice:

In your journal, write the heading: "My Cleansed Portal."

Write this declaration:

"God has sanctified my history. My portal is cleansed. My

scars are proof of the Surgeon's skill. I am not ashamed. I am whole. I am free."

Read it aloud.

Place your hand over your heart. Say: "My portal is cleansed. I am whole."

Your Frequency Work: A cleansed portal vibrates at a pure, holy frequency, like water washing over stone. As you speak, notice the clarity, the peace, the sense of being made new. That's the frequency of sanctification. Say: "My portal is cleansed. I am holy." Feel the shift.

The Liturgy (Speak aloud): "My portal is cleansed. God has sanctified my history. My scars are proof of His skill. I am not ashamed. I am whole. I am holy. I am free."

Authority Declaration: "My portal is cleansed. I am not ashamed."

Journaling Prompt:

What does it mean for your portal to be cleansed?

How does this change the way you see your history?

Closing Prayer: "Jesus, my portal is cleansed. Thank You for sanctifying my history. I am whole. I am holy. I am Yours. Amen."

Day 24: Building Your Testimony

Today's Focus: Your testimony is weaponized evidence. Today, you begin to build your testimony, the story of how the Seventh Man set you free.

The Practice:

In your journal, write the heading: "My Testimony."

Answer these questions:

Where were you before the Seventh Man met you?

What did He do to set you free?

Where are you now?

Write your testimony in 3-5 sentences. Keep it simple. Keep it true.

Read it aloud. This is your weapon.

Your Frequency Work: Testimony vibrates at a powerful, declarative frequency, like a trumpet announcing victory. As you speak, notice the authority, the clarity, the sense of being a witness. That's the frequency of testimony. Say: "This is my testimony. This is how I got free." Feel the shift.

The Liturgy (Speak aloud): "This is my testimony. The Seventh Man set me free. I was bound, but now I am free. I was ashamed, but now I am whole. This is my weapon. This is my evidence."

Authority Declaration: "My testimony is a weapon. I am a witness."

Journaling Prompt:

What is your testimony?

Who needs to hear it?

Closing Prayer: "Jesus, this is my testimony. Thank You for setting me free. Use my story to set others free. I am Yours. Amen."

Day 25: The Dabeq Frequency Work

Today's Focus: If you are married, today you practice the Dabeq frequency, the holy fusion of two souls into one. If you are single, today you establish the frequency you will carry into covenant.

The Practice (Married):

Sit with your spouse. Hold hands.

Pray together: "Jesus, we invite You into our covenant. We are not just two people—we are one flesh, fused by Your design. Establish the Dabeq frequency in us. Guard our portal. Sustain our fusion."

Speak a blessing over your spouse: "I honor you. I cleave to you. I am fused to you. We are one."

Sit in silence for 5 minutes. Feel the frequency.

The Practice (Single):

Sit in silence. Place your hand over your heart.

Pray: "Jesus, I am preparing for covenant. Establish the frequency in me now. Teach me to honor, to cleave, to fuse. Prepare me for the one You have for me."

Declare aloud: "I am establishing the Dabeq frequency. I am preparing for covenant. I am whole."

Your Frequency Work: Dabeq vibrates at a harmonious, unified frequency—like two instruments playing in perfect harmony. As you practice, notice the peace, the unity, the sense of being held. That's the frequency of covenant. Say: "We are one. We are fused. We are His." Feel the shift.

The Liturgy (Speak aloud):"We are one flesh. We are fused by the Seventh Man. We vibrate at the Dabeq frequency. We are holy. We are whole. We are His."

Authority Declaration: "We have authority to establish the Dabeq frequency. We are one."

Journaling Prompt:

What does the Dabeq frequency feel like?

How will you maintain it?

Closing Prayer: "Jesus, establish the Dabeq frequency in us. Guard our portal. Sustain our fusion. We are one. We are Yours. Amen."

Day 26: Generational Blessing Declarations

Today's Focus: Today, you release blessing to your descendants. You declare that the cycle is broken, the frequency is shifted, and the portal is open for generational healing.

The Practice:

In your journal, write the heading: "Generational Blessing."

Write a blessing for your children (or future children). Examples:

"I declare that my children will inherit the frequency of the Seventh Man, not the frequency of the Five."

"I declare that my children will walk in wholeness, not shame."

"I declare that my children will be covenant-keepers, not curse-carriers."

Read it aloud with authority.

Declare aloud: "I am a generational healer. I break the cycle. I release blessing."

Your Frequency Work: Generational blessing vibrates at a flowing, expansive frequency, like a river running forward. As you speak, notice the sense of legacy, the weight of responsibility, the joy of healing. That's the frequency of generational blessing. Say: "I release blessing. I am a healer." Feel the shift.

The Liturgy (Speak aloud): "I am a generational healer. I break the cycle. I release blessing to my descendants. They will inherit the frequency of the Seventh Man. They will walk in wholeness. They will be free."

Authority Declaration: "I have authority to release generational blessing. I am a healer."

Journaling Prompt:

What blessing are you releasing to your descendants?

What will they inherit from you?

Closing Prayer: "Jesus, I release blessing to my descendants. Break the cycle. Establish a new pattern. They are Yours. Amen."

Day 27: The Open Portal of Blessing

Today's Focus: You have spent weeks closing portals. Today, you open a portal, a portal of blessing, healing, and generational restoration. You are not just breaking cycles; you are establishing new ones.

The Practice:

In your journal, write the heading: "The Open Portal of Blessing."

Write this declaration:

"I open a portal of blessing over my life, my marriage, my family, my lineage. This portal flows backward to my ancestors and forward to my descendants. I am a healer. I am a blessing-carrier. I am free."

Read it aloud with authority.

Declare aloud: "I open the portal of blessing. I am a healer."

Your Frequency Work: An open portal of blessing vibrates at a radiant, life-giving frequency, like light pouring through a window. As you speak, notice the warmth, the joy, the sense of abundance. That's the frequency of blessing. Say: "I open the portal. I am a blessing." Feel the shift.

The Liturgy (Speak aloud):"I open a portal of blessing. This portal flows backward and forward. I am a healer. I am a blessing-carrier. I am free."

Authority Declaration: "I have authority to open portals of blessing. I am a healer."

Journaling Prompt:

What does it feel like to open a portal of blessing?

Who will be blessed by this portal?

Closing Prayer: "Jesus, I open a portal of blessing. Flow through me. Heal through me. Bless through me. I am Yours. Amen."

Day 28: Authority Confirmation

Today's Focus: Today, you confirm the authority you've reclaimed. You are not a victim. You are a steward. You have dominion over your soul, your portals, your frequency, your covenant.

The Practice:

In your journal, write the heading: "Authority Confirmation."

Write this declaration:

"I, [your name], confirm the authority I have reclaimed. I have dominion over my soul. I decide which portals stay open. I decide which frequencies I vibrate at. I decide which covenants I honor. I am not a victim. I am a steward. I am a New Creation. I am free."

Read it aloud with conviction.

Stand up. Place your hand over your heart. Say: "I have

authority. I am free."

Your Frequency Work: Authority vibrates at a steady, unshakable frequency, like a foundation. As you speak, notice the strength, the clarity, the sense of dominion. That's the frequency of authority. Say: "I have authority. I am free." Feel the shift.

The Liturgy (Speak aloud): "I confirm the authority I have reclaimed. I have dominion over my soul. I am not a victim. I am a steward. I am a New Creation. I am free."

Authority Declaration: "I have authority over my soul. I am not going back."

Journaling Prompt:

What does it feel like to confirm your authority?

How will you steward this authority moving forward?

Closing Prayer: "Jesus, I confirm the authority I have reclaimed. Thank You for restoring my dominion. I am a steward. I am free. I am Yours. Amen."

Day 29: Preparing for the Altar

Today's Focus: Tomorrow, you will seal the entire 30-day journey with a comprehensive covenant prayer. Today, you prepare your heart for the altar.

The Practice:

In your journal, write the heading: "Preparing for the Altar."

Reflect on the past 29 days. Write:

What has God healed in you?

What has shifted?

What are you leaving behind?

What are you stepping into?

Write this declaration: "I am ready for the altar. I am ready to seal the covenant. I am ready to step into daily restoration."

Sit in silence for 5 minutes. Prepare your heart.

Your Frequency Work: Preparation vibrates at a reverent, anticipatory frequency, like the moment before a wedding. As you sit in silence, notice the sense of readiness, the weight of the moment, the joy of what's coming. That's the frequency of preparation. Say: "I am ready. I am His." Feel the shift.

The Liturgy (Speak aloud):"I am ready for the altar. I am ready to seal the covenant. I am ready to step into daily restoration. I am His."

Authority Declaration: "I am ready. I am not going back."

Journaling Prompt:

What has God healed in you over the past 29 days?

What are you stepping into tomorrow?

Closing Prayer: "Jesus, I am ready for the altar. Prepare my heart. I am Yours. Amen."

Day 30: The Altar of Restoration

Today's Focus: Today, you seal the entire 30-day journey with a comprehensive covenant prayer. This is not the end; it's the beginning of daily restoration.

The Practice:

Find a quiet place. Kneel if you are able.

Pray this covenant prayer aloud (or write your own):

"Jesus, Seventh Man, Healer of my soul—

I come to the altar today to seal the covenant You have made with me.

I acknowledge the Five Husbands. I bring them to You. I cannot heal this alone, but You can. I renounce every unholy covenant I entered. I close every portal I opened. I return every lie I believed. I take back every piece of my soul that was stolen.

I renounce the Mother of Shame. I divorce her voice. I am not ashamed. I am beloved.

I renounce the Father of Lust. I divorce his pattern. I am not a consumer. I am a covenant-keeper.

I return the generational inheritance of lies. I break the ancestral altar. I am not bound by my ancestors' choices. I am a generational healer.

I acknowledge the weight of the Five. I give it to You. I cannot carry it anymore. Take it. Close the portals. Set me free.

I am a New Creation. Old things have passed away. All things have become new. I am not recovering. I am transformed. I am whole. I am free.

My portal is cleansed. God has sanctified my history. My scars are proof of His skill. I am not ashamed.

I have authority over my own soul. I decide which portals stay open. I decide which frequencies I vibrate at. I decide which covenants I honor. I am not a victim. I am a steward.

I open a portal of blessing over my life, my marriage, my family, my lineage. This portal flows backward to my ancestors and forward to my descendants. I am a healer. I am a blessing-carrier.

I seal this covenant with the Blood of Jesus. I am cleaved, Dabeq, to the Seventh Man. I am fused to Him. I vibrate at His frequency. I am His.

I am not going back. I am stepping forward. I am walking in daily restoration.

In the name of Jesus, the Seventh Man, the Healer of my soul, Amen."

Sit in silence for 10 minutes. Let the covenant settle into your soul.

Stand up. Place your hand over your heart. Say: "I am sealed. I am His. I am free."

Your Frequency Work: The altar vibrates at a sacred, sealing frequency, like a covenant being signed. As you pray, notice the weight, the reverence, the sense of finality. That's the frequency of covenant. Say: "I am sealed. I am His." Feel the shift.

The Liturgy (Speak aloud): "I am sealed. I am His. I am free. I am not going back. I am stepping forward. I am walking in daily restoration."

Authority Declaration: "I am sealed in the covenant. I am not going back."

Journaling Prompt:

What does it feel like to seal the covenant?

What are you stepping into now?

Closing Prayer: "Jesus, I am sealed. I am His. I am free. Thank You for the past 30 days. Thank You for the healing. Thank You for the restoration. I am Yours. Amen."

What Comes Next: Daily Restoration

The 30 days are complete. But the work is not over.

This is not the end. This is the beginning of daily restoration.

Every day, you will maintain the altar. Every day, you will practice the liturgies. Every day, you will walk in the authority you've reclaimed. Every day, you will vibrate at the frequency of the Seventh Man.

This is not a grind. This is not bondage. This is the rhythm of freedom.

The Seventh Man meets you here. Every single day.

You are not going back.

You are stepping forward.

You are walking in daily restoration.

Welcome to the rest of your life.

APPENDICES

APPENDIX A: SCRIPTURE INDEX

This index organizes the biblical foundation for the teachings in Sexual Healing. These are not proof-texts—they are the theological architecture upon which the entire book is built. Use this index to deepen your understanding, to study the Word for yourself, and to ground your healing in the authority of Scripture.

COVENANT & BLOOD COVENANT

Genesis 2:24 — "Therefore shall a man leave his father and his mother, and shall cleave unto his wife: and they shall be one flesh." The foundational verse for understanding covenant marriage. "One flesh" is not a metaphor; it's spiritual mechanics. This is the blueprint for Dabeq (cleaving) and the reason sexual union outside covenant creates binding.

Genesis 15:9-18 — Abraham's blood covenant with God. Blood was shed, animals were cut in half, and God walked between the pieces. This establishes the pattern: covenant requires blood, and a blood covenant is unbreakable. Every sexual encounter is a blood covenant, whether you intended it or not.

Hebrews 9:22 — "Without shedding of blood is no remission."

Blood is the currency of covenant. This is why sex is never "just sex"; it involves the shedding of blood (hymen, menstruation, or spiritual exchange). Blood opens portals and establishes legal rights.

1 Corinthians 6:16 — "What? know ye not that he which is joined to a harlot is one body? for two, saith he, shall be one flesh." Paul confirms that sexual union, even outside marriage, creates "one flesh" binding. This is the Cumulative Covenant Effect in action. Every partner you've been with, you're still "one" with, until the covenant is severed.

Matthew 26:28 — "For this is my blood of the new testament, which is shed for many for the remission of sins." Jesus establishes the New Covenant in His blood. This is the only blood powerful enough to break unholy covenants and cleanse defiled portals. The Seventh Man's blood is the key to your freedom.

Exodus 24:8 — Moses sprinkled the blood of the covenant on the people. Blood seals covenant. Blood opens doors. Blood grants access. This is why sexual sin is not just "moral failure," it's covenant violation with spiritual consequences.

Malachi 2:14 — "The LORD hath been witness between thee and the wife of thy youth, against whom thou hast dealt treacherously: yet is she thy companion, and the wife of thy covenant." God Himself is the witness to the covenant. When you break a covenant (through adultery, fornication, or abandonment), you're not just hurting a person; you're violating a three-party agreement with God as guarantor.

Ephesians 5:31-32 — "For this cause shall a man leave his father and mother, and shall be joined unto his wife, and the two shall be one flesh. This is a great mystery: but I speak concerning Christ and the church." Marriage is the earthly picture of Christ's covenant with the Church. This is why sexual purity matters; it's not just about behavior; it's about reflecting the sacred mystery of divine union.

SEXUALITY & DESIGN

1 Corinthians 6:18 — "Flee fornication. Every sin that a man doeth is without the body; but he that committeth fornication sinneth against his own body." Sexual sin is unique; it's a sin against your own body. This is because your body is a temple, and sexual sin defiles the sanctuary. It's not just external, it's an internal violation.

1 Thessalonians 4:3-5 — "For this is the will of God, even your sanctification, that ye should abstain from fornication: That every one of you should know how to possess his vessel in sanctification and honour; Not in the lust of concupiscence,

even as the Gentiles which know not God." God's will is your sanctification, and that includes your sexuality. You are called to "possess your vessel" (your body, your soul) in honor, not lust.

Proverbs 5:15-19 — "Drink waters out of thine own cistern, and running waters out of thine own well... Let thy fountain be blessed: and rejoice with the wife of thy youth." God's design for sexuality is exclusive, covenantal, and life-giving. Your "cistern" and "well" are meant for one person, your covenant partner. Drinking from broken cisterns (outside covenant) leads to defilement and death.

Song of Solomon 4:12 — "A garden inclosed is my sister, my spouse; a spring shut up, a fountain sealed." The bride's body is described as "enclosed," "shut up," "sealed," protected, sacred, and reserved. This is the opposite of the world's "55s" that teach your body is public property. Your sexuality is a sanctuary, not a commodity.

Hebrews 13:4 — "Marriage is honourable in all, and the bed undefiled: but whoremongers and adulterers God will judge." The marriage bed is holy, undefiled. But sexual sin (fornication, adultery) brings judgment. This is not condemnation, it's consequence. God judges because covenant violation has a real spiritual impact.

1 Corinthians 7:4 — "The wife hath not power of her own body, but the husband: and likewise, also the husband hath not power of his own body, but the wife." In a covenant, you surrender authority over your own body to your spouse. This is the Dabeq frequency, mutual submission, mutual authority, mutual fusion. Outside the covenant, this becomes bondage and control.

Romans 1:24-27 — Paul describes the consequences of rejecting God's design for sexuality: "God gave them up unto uncleanness through the lusts of their own hearts, to dishonour their own bodies between themselves." When we reject God's design, we dishonor our own bodies. This is the "55s" in action—cultural lies that lead to self-destruction.

Genesis 1:27-28 — "So God created man in his own image, in the image of God created he him; male and female created he them. And God blessed them, and God said unto them, Be fruitful, and multiply." Sexuality is part of the image of God; it's creative, generative, life-giving. This is bara (what God made you to be), not asa (what shame says you are).

IDENTITY & TRANSFORMATION (ASA VS. BARA)

2 Corinthians 5:17 — "Therefore if any man be in Christ, he is a new creature: old things are passed away; behold, all things

are become new." This is the foundation of New Creation identity. You are not "recovering," you are transformed. Old things (asa, what you've done) have passed away. All things (bara, what God made you to be) have become new.

Ephesians 4:22-24 — "That ye put off concerning the former conversation the old man, which is corrupt according to the deceitful lusts; And be renewed in the spirit of your mind; And that ye put on the new man, which after God is created in righteousness and true holiness." You are called to "put off" the old identity (shame, lust, lies) and "put on" the new identity (righteousness, holiness, truth). This is the work of the Spiritual Bill of Divorcement.

Romans 12:2 — "And be not conformed to this world: but be ye transformed by the renewing of your mind, that ye may prove what is that good, and acceptable, and perfect, will of God." Transformation happens in the mind first. This is why interrupting the fantasy (2 Corinthians 10:5) is so critical; the battle is won or lost in the thought life.

Colossians 3:9-10 — "Lie not one to another, seeing that ye have put off the old man with his deeds; And have put on the new man, which is renewed in knowledge after the image of him that created him." The "new man" is renewed in the image of God; this is bara. The "old man" is defined by deeds, this is asa. You are not what you've done. You are what God made you to be.

Isaiah 43:18-19 — "Remember ye not the former things, neither consider the things of old. Behold, I will do a new thing; now it shall spring forth; shall ye not know it? I will even make a way in the wilderness, and rivers in the desert." God is doing a new thing, not just fixing the old thing. This is the promise of the Wilderness season: discomfort is preparation for the new.
Psalm 139:13-14 — "For thou hast possessed my reins: thou hast covered me in my mother's womb. I will praise thee; for I am fearfully and wonderfully made." This is bara, what God made you to be. You were fearfully and wonderfully made before you ever sinned, before you ever opened a portal, before you ever absorbed a "55." Your identity is rooted in God's design, not your history.
Jeremiah 1:5 — "Before I formed thee in the belly I knew thee; and before thou camest forth out of the womb I sanctified thee." God knew you and sanctified you before you were born. This means your identity precedes your actions. Asa (what you've done) does not define you. Bara (what God made you to be) is your true identity.

Galatians 2:20 — "I am crucified with Christ: nevertheless I live; yet not I, but Christ liveth in me: and the life which I now live in the flesh I live by the faith of the Son of God, who loved me, and gave himself for me." Your old identity is crucified. The life you live now is Christ in you. This is the New Creation, not self-improvement, but complete transformation.

SPIRITUAL AUTHORITY & DOMINION

Luke 10:19 — "Behold, I give unto you power to tread on serpents and scorpions, and over all the power of the enemy: and nothing shall by any means hurt you." Jesus gives you authority over the enemy. This is not theoretical, it's legal, spiritual authority. You have the right to tread on serpents (lies, lust, shame) and scorpions (generational habits, demonic oppression). Nothing can hurt you when you walk in this authority.

Matthew 16:19 — "And I will give unto thee the keys of the kingdom of heaven: and whatsoever thou shalt bind on earth shall be bound in heaven: and whatsoever thou shalt loose on earth shall be loosed in heaven." You have the authority to bind and loose, to close portals and open portals, to sever covenants and establish covenants. This is the authority you reclaim in Chapter 6.

James 4:7 — "Submit yourselves therefore to God. Resist the devil, and he will flee from you." Resistance requires submission first. You cannot resist the devil in your own strength; you must submit to God, walk in His authority, and then resist. When you do, the devil flees. This is high-frequency warfare.

Ephesians 6:12 — "For we wrestle not against flesh and blood, but against principalities, against power, against the rulers of the darkness of this world, against spiritual wickedness in high places." The battle is not against people, it's against spiritual forces. This is why sexual healing requires spiritual warfare, not just therapy. You're not fighting your ex-partner, you're fighting the principalities that gained access through the portal.

2 Corinthians 10:4-5 — "For the weapons of our warfare are not carnal, but mighty through God to the pulling down of strong holds; Casting down imaginations, and every high thing that exalteth itself against the knowledge of God, and bringing into captivity every thought to the obedience of Christ." This is the foundation for interrupting the fantasy. You have the authority to cast down imaginations, to take every thought captive. The battle is won in the mind.

1 John 4:4 — "Ye are of God, little children, and have overcome them: because greater is he that is in you, than he that is in the world." The Spirit in you is greater than the enemy

in the world. This is your authority—not because of your strength, but because of His strength in you.

Revelation 12:11 — "And they overcame him by the blood of the Lamb, and by the word of their testimony; and they loved not their lives unto the death." You overcome by two things: the blood of Jesus (covenant authority) and the word of your testimony (weaponized evidence). Your story is not just personal, it's a weapon that breaks strongholds.

Colossians 2:15 — "And having spoiled principalities and powers, he made a shew of them openly, triumphing over them in it." Jesus has already defeated the enemy. You're not fighting for victory—you're fighting from victory. The enemy has no legal right to you unless you give it to him through open portals.

GENERATIONAL BLESSING & HABITS

Exodus 20:5-6 — "For I the LORD thy God am a jealous God, visiting the iniquity of the fathers upon the children unto the third and fourth generation of them that hate me; And shewing mercy unto thousands of them that love me, and keep my commandments." Generational patterns are real. Sin creates generational habits that pass down through bloodlines. But obedience creates generational blessing that extends to thousands. This is why your healing matters, you're not just healing yourself; you're healing your lineage.

Deuteronomy 28:1-14 — The blessings of obedience. When you walk in covenant with God, blessing flows to your children, your work, your body, and your land. This is the open portal of blessing, what you establish generationally when you walk in wholeness.

Deuteronomy 28:15-68 — The curses of disobedience. When you break a covenant, curses follow, disease, poverty, oppression, and confusion. This is not God punishing you; it's the natural consequence of stepping outside His protection. Generational habits are broken when you renounce the covenant and return to God's design.

Galatians 3:13-14 — "Christ hath redeemed us from the curse of the law, being made a curse for us: for it is written, Cursed is every one that hangeth on a tree: That the blessing of Abraham might come on the Gentiles through Jesus Christ." Jesus broke the curse on the cross. You are no longer under the curse, you are under the blessing. This is the authority you walk in when you sever ties with the Ancestral Altar.

Proverbs 22:6 — "Train up a child in the way he should go: and when he is old, he will not depart from it." What you establish in your children becomes their inheritance. This is why the Dabeq frequency matters, your children inherit the frequency you establish in your covenant.

Psalm 103:17-18 — "But the mercy of the LORD is from everlasting to everlasting upon them that fear him, and his righteousness unto children's children; To such as keep his covenant, and to those that remember his commandments to do them." Covenant obedience creates generational righteousness. Your healing becomes your children's inheritance.

Lamentations 5:7 — "Our fathers have sinned, and are not; and we have borne their iniquities." This is the Generational Backpack, the weight of inherited sin and trauma. But you have the authority to set it down and refuse to carry what your ancestors chose.

Ezekiel 18:20 — "The soul that sinneth, it shall die. The son shall not bear the iniquity of the father, neither shall the father bear the iniquity of the son." You are not doomed to repeat your parents' patterns. You have the authority to break the cycle. This is the promise of generational healing.

HEALING & RESTORATION

Psalm 147:3 — "He healeth the broken in heart, and bindeth

up their wounds." God is the Healer of the brokenhearted. This is not just emotional comfort, it's spiritual restoration. He binds up wounds that no human can heal.

Isaiah 61:1-3 — "The Spirit of the Lord GOD is upon me; because the LORD hath anointed me to preach good tidings unto the meek; he hath sent me to bind up the brokenhearted, to proclaim liberty to the captives, and the opening of the prison to them that are bound... to give unto them beauty for ashes, the oil of joy for mourning, the garment of praise for the spirit of heaviness." This is the Seventh Man's mission, to heal, to liberate, to restore. Beauty for ashes. Joy for mourning. Praise for heaviness. This is the altar of restoration.

Jeremiah 30:17 — "For I will restore health unto thee, and I will heal thee of thy wounds, saith the LORD." God promises restoration. Not just recovery, restoration. He doesn't just stop the bleeding; He makes you whole.

Joel 2:25 — "And I will restore to you the years that the locust hath eaten." God restores what was stolen. The years lost to addiction, shame, lust, trauma, God redeems them. This is the cleansed portal, God sanctifying your history and turning it into a weapon.

Ezekiel 36:26 — "A new heart also will I give you, and a new spirit will I put within you: and I will take away the stony heart out of your flesh, and I will give you an heart of flesh." God doesn't just repair the old heart, He gives you a new heart. This is New Creation identity. You are not recovering; you are transformed.

Psalm 51:10 — "Create in me a clean heart, O God; and renew a right spirit within me." David's prayer after his sin with Bathsheba. This is the prayer of the Woman at the Well, "Create in me a clean heart." Not "fix my heart," create a clean heart. This is bara, not asa.

Isaiah 43:25 — "I, even I, am he that blotteth out thy transgressions for mine own sake, and will not remember thy sins." God doesn't just forgive, He forgets. He blots out your transgressions. This is the promise of the cleansed portal: your history is sanctified, not erased, but redeemed.

1 Peter 2:24 — "Who his own self bare our sins in his own body on the tree, that we, being dead to sins, should live unto righteousness: by whose stripes ye were healed." Healing is not just spiritual, it's physical, emotional, and generational. By His stripes, you were healed. Past tense. The healing is already done. You're just stepping into it.

SPIRITUAL WARFARE

Ephesians 6:10-18 — The full armor of God. This is the foundation for high-frequency warfare. You are called to stand, to wrestle, to fight, not in your own strength, but in the strength of the Lord. The armor is truth, righteousness, the gospel, faith, salvation, the Word, and prayer. This is how you maintain the altar.

2 Corinthians 10:3-5 — "For though we walk in the flesh, we do not war after the flesh: (For the weapons of our warfare are not carnal, but mighty through God to the pulling down of strong holds;) Casting down imaginations, and every high thing that exalteth itself against the knowledge of God, and bringing into captivity every thought to the obedience of Christ." This is the key to breaking the addiction cycle, casting down imaginations. The battle is in the mind.

1 Peter 5:8 — "Be sober, be vigilant; because your adversary the devil, as a roaring lion, walketh about, seeking whom he may devour." The enemy is real, and he is hunting. But he can only devour those who give him access. Close the portals, and he has no legal right to you.

John 10:10 — "The thief cometh not, but for to steal, and to kill, and to destroy: I am come that they might have life, and that they might have it more abundantly." The enemy's mission is theft, death, and destruction. Jesus' mission is life, abundant, overflowing, generational life. This is the choice: the thief or the Seventh Man.

Isaiah 54:17 — "No weapon that is formed against thee shall prosper; and every tongue that shall rise against thee in judgment thou shalt condemn. This is the heritage of the servants of the LORD, and their righteousness is of me, saith the LORD." You have the authority to condemn every lie, every accusation, every "55" that rises against you. No weapon formed against you will prosper.

Psalm 91:1-16 — The promise of divine protection. "He that dwelleth in the secret place of the most High shall abide under the shadow of the Almighty." When you walk in covenant with God, you are protected. The enemy cannot touch you without permission.

PRAYER & INTERCESSION

1 Thessalonians 5:17 — "Pray without ceasing." Prayer is not an event, it's a lifestyle. This is the rhythm of daily restoration. You maintain the altar through constant communion with the Seventh Man.

Matthew 6:6 — "But thou, when thou prayest, enter into thy

closet, and when thou hast shut thy door, pray to thy Father which is in secret; and thy Father which seeth in secret shall reward thee openly." Prayer is intimate, secret, personal. This is where the Seventh Man meets you, in the closet, in the Wilderness, in the silence.

Romans 8:26 — "Likewise the Spirit also helpeth our infirmities: for we know not what we should pray for as we ought: but the Spirit itself maketh intercession for us with groanings which cannot be uttered." When you don't have words, the Spirit prays for you. This is the frequency work, feeling the shift even when you can't articulate it.

James 5:16 — "Confess your faults one to another, and pray one for another, that ye may be healed. The effectual fervent prayer of a righteous man availeth much." Healing happens in community. This is why the Small Group Leader Guide matters—you are not meant to walk this journey alone.

Philippians 4:6-7 — "Be careful for nothing; but in every thing by prayer and supplication with thanksgiving let your requests be made known unto God. And the peace of God, which passeth all understanding, shall keep your hearts and minds through Christ Jesus." Prayer brings peace. This is the frequency shift, from anxiety to peace, from chaos to rest.

THE WOMAN AT THE WELL & JESUS' TEACHINGS

John 4:1-42 — The entire narrative of the Woman at the Well. This is the primary teaching metaphor for the book. The Five Husbands (past covenants), the One (current relationship), the Seventh Man (Jesus), the diagnostic moment ("Go, call thy husband"), the cleansed portal (leaving the waterpot), the testimony (provoking the city). This is the blueprint for sexual healing.

John 4:13-14 — "Jesus answered and said unto her, Whosoever drinketh of this water shall thirst again: But whosoever drinketh of the water that I shall give him shall never thirst; but the water that I shall give him shall be in him a well of water springing up into everlasting life." The Seventh Man offers living water, not temporary satisfaction, but eternal fulfillment. This is the difference between lust (temporary) and covenant (eternal).

John 8:3-11 — The woman caught in adultery. "Neither do I condemn thee: go, and sin no more." The Seventh Man does not condemn, He restores. But restoration requires repentance ("go, and sin no more"). This is the balance of grace and truth.

Matthew 5:27-28 — "Ye have heard that it was said by them of old time, Thou shalt not commit adultery: But I say unto you,

That whosoever looketh on a woman to lust after her hath committed adultery with her already in his heart." The battle is in the mind. Lust is not just action, it's imagination. This is why interrupting the fantasy is so critical.

John 3:16-17 — "For God so loved the world, that he gave his only begotten Son, that whosoever believeth in him should not perish, but have everlasting life. For God sent not his Son into the world to condemn the world; but that the world through him might be saved." The Seventh Man came to save, not condemn. This is the heart of the gospel, and the heart of sexual healing.

NEW CREATION

2 Corinthians 5:17 — "Therefore if any man be in Christ, he is a new creature: old things are passed away; behold, all things are become new." The foundation of New Creation identity. You are not recovering, you are transformed.

Galatians 6:15 — "For in Christ Jesus neither circumcision availeth anything, nor uncircumcision, but a new creature." Your past does not define you. Your actions do not define you. You are a New Creation.

Ephesians 2:10 — "For we are his workmanship, created in Christ Jesus unto good works, which God hath before ordained that we should walk in them." You are God's workmanship, His masterpiece. You were created for good works, not shame. This is bara, what God made you to be.

Revelation 21:5 — "And he that sat upon the throne said, Behold, I make all things new. And he said unto me, Write: for these words are true and faithful." God makes all things new. Not some things. Not most things. All things. This is the promise of the altar of restoration.

Isaiah 43:19 — "Behold, I will do a new thing; now it shall spring forth; shall ye not know it? I will even make a way in the wilderness, and rivers in the desert." God is doing a new thing, right now, in the Wilderness, in the discomfort. The new thing is already springing forth.

Use this Scripture Index as a foundation for your healing journey. These are not just verses; they are the authority upon which your freedom is built. Study them. Memorize them. Declare them. Let the Word of God become the frequency you vibrate at.

The Seventh Man meets you in the Word. Every single day.

APPENDIX B: GLOSSARY OF KEY TERMS

This glossary defines the 24 core concepts and metaphors used throughout Sexual Healing. These are not abstract theological ideas; they are the spiritual mechanics of your healing. Use this as a reference guide whenever you encounter a term and need clarity on its meaning and application.

Asa vs. Bara

Asa is what you have done—your actions, your history, your shame. It is the accumulation of choices, mistakes, and entanglements. Bara is what God made you to be, your true identity, your design, your purpose. The core teaching of this book is that asa does not define bara. You are not what you've done; you are what God created you to be. Healing happens when you stop believing the lie that your history is your identity.

Used in context: Chapter 2 (The Mechanics of the Soul), Chapter 3 (The Diagnostic Moment), Chapter 7 (The Altar of Restoration), Workbook Weeks 1-4

Ancestral Altar

The inherited patterns, generational trauma, and family system dysfunction that you carry in your bloodline. This is not just psychological—it is spiritual. The Ancestral Altar is the place where your ancestors' choices, covenants, and curses are still active in your life. Breaking free requires renouncing the agreements your family made and refusing to carry what was not yours to carry.

Used in context: Chapter 4 (The Art of Leaving), Workbook Week 2 (Days 11-12)

Authority (Spiritual)

Your legitimate dominion and power in Christ to command your own soul, close spiritual portals, sever unholy covenants, and establish new frequencies. Authority is not something you earn or deserve; it is your inheritance as a child of God. You have the authority to bind and loose, to resist the enemy, and to reclaim what was stolen. This authority is grounded in the blood of Jesus and the Word of God.

Used in context: Chapter 6 (The Ritual of the Soul), Chapter 7 (The Altar of Restoration), Workbook Weeks 3-4, Authority Declarations throughout

Blood Covenant

A binding spiritual agreement sealed by the shedding of blood. In Scripture, a blood covenant is the most serious form of agreement; it is unbreakable and involves the entire being of both parties. Sexual union is a blood covenant because it involves the shedding of blood (hymen, menstruation, or spiritual exchange). Every sexual encounter outside of marriage creates a blood covenant with that person, whether you intended it or not. This is why sex is never "just sex."

Used in context: Chapter 2 (The Mechanics of the Soul), Chapter 3 (The Diagnostic Moment), Scripture Index

Cleaving / Dabeq Frequency

Cleaving is the biblical term for the spiritual fusion that happens in covenant marriage (Genesis 2:24). Dabeq is the Hebrew word meaning "to cling, to adhere, to be joined." The Dabeq Frequency is God's design for two people to become spiritually fused—not codependent, but powerfully aligned. True cleaving requires that you have first left (severed ties with family systems and past covenants). Cleaving is the power of two becoming one without losing individual identity.

Used in context: Chapter 5 (The Power of Cleaving), Workbook Week 4 (Days 25, 27)

Cumulative Covenant Effect

The spiritual reality that every sexual partner you've been with creates a binding that affects your present relationships. When you enter a new relationship, you bring all your past partners' imprints, frequencies, and spiritual entanglements with you. This is why "the One cannot fix the Five"—your current partner cannot heal what multiple past covenants have created. Breaking the Cumulative Covenant Effect requires severing ties with all past partners and renouncing the agreements made with them.

Used in context: Chapter 2 (The Mechanics of the Soul), Chapter 3 (The Diagnostic Moment), Workbook Week 1 (Days 1, 6)

Father of Lust

The internalized voice and pattern of false sexuality, perversion of desire, and control. The Father of Lust is the demonic/cultural voice that teaches you to use sexuality as a weapon, a transaction, or an escape. He teaches men to conquer and women to perform. He teaches that desire is shameful or that desire justifies any action. Severing ties with the Father of Lust requires renouncing lust patterns and reclaiming sexuality as sacred, not shameful.

Used in context: Chapter 4 (The Art of Leaving), Workbook Week 2 (Days 11, 14)

Five Husbands

The metaphor from John 4 (Woman at the Well) representing past sexual/covenantal entanglements. The Woman at the Well had five husbands and was currently with a sixth man who was not her husband. These represent the Cumulative Covenant Effect—multiple past partners who still have spiritual claim on her. Your "Five Husbands" are your past sexual partners whose covenants must be renounced and severed before you can fully cleave to your current or future partner.

Used in context: Chapter 3 (The Diagnostic Moment), Workbook Week 1 (Day 1)

Frequency

The spiritual vibration or resonance that you emit based on your beliefs, choices, and covenants. Everything vibrates at a frequency—shame vibrates low, truth vibrates high. Your frequency attracts or repels; it opens or closes doors; it creates generational portals. When you shift your frequency from shame to authority, from lust to wholeness, from death to life, you literally change the spiritual atmosphere around you. This is why "frequency work" is central to the 30-day workbook.

Used in context: Throughout all chapters, Workbook Weeks 1-4, especially Week 2 (Day 14) and Week 4

Generational Blessing

The inheritance of wholeness, righteousness, and favor that flows to your children and descendants when you walk in covenant with God. Generational blessing is not just emotional—it is spiritual and practical. When you heal your sexual history, break generational habits, and establish new frequencies, you create an open portal of blessing for your lineage. Your children inherit what you establish.

Used in context: Chapter 5 (The Power of Cleaving), Chapter 7 (The Altar of Restoration), Workbook Week 4 (Days 26-27), Scripture Index

Generational Habit

The inheritance of dysfunction, trauma, and spiritual bondage that flows to your children and descendants when unholy covenants and patterns are left unbroken. generational habits are real—they pass through bloodlines and affect multiple generations. Sexual sin, broken covenants, and unhealed trauma create generational habits that your children inherit unless you break the cycle. This is why your healing is not just personal—it is generational.

Used in context: Chapter 4 (The Art of Leaving), Chapter 5 (The Power of Cleaving), Scripture Index

Generational Portal

A spiritual opening or gateway created by the patterns you establish in your life that your children inherit. If you establish a portal of shame, lust, and broken covenant, your children inherit access to that portal. If you establish a portal of wholeness, authority, and cleansed sexuality, your children inherit blessing. Your healing literally changes the spiritual inheritance of your lineage.

Used in context: Chapter 5 (The Power of Cleaving), Chapter 7 (The Altar of Restoration), Workbook Week 4 (Days 26-27)

Generational Trauma

The inherited psychological, emotional, and spiritual wounds passed down through family systems. Generational trauma is not just "learned behavior"—it is spiritual inheritance. Your parents' unhealed wounds, your grandparents' broken covenants, your ancestors' survival patterns—all of these live in your nervous system and your spirit. Healing generational trauma requires understanding both the psychological and spiritual roots.

Used in context: Chapter 4 (The Art of Leaving), Workbook Week 1 (Day 5)

High-Frequency Warfare

Spiritual authority work that involves speaking truth into the atmosphere, declaring dominion over your own soul, and shifting frequencies through prayer, declaration, and presence. High-frequency warfare is not aggressive or violent—it is the calm, confident assertion of truth in the face of lies. It is speaking from dominion, not from need. It is the practice of maintaining the altar through daily spiritual disciplines.

Used in context: Chapter 6 (The Ritual of the Soul), Workbook Week 3 (Day 20), Workbook Week 4

Lust

The perversion of desire that seeks to use, control, or escape rather than to love, serve, or connect. Lust is not the same as desire—desire is God-given and sacred. Lust is desire twisted into a weapon, a transaction, or an addiction. Lust opens portals to demonic influence and creates spiritual bondage. Breaking lust requires interrupting the fantasy, starving the ritual, and converting death rituals into life liturgies.

Used in context: Chapter 1 (The Con), Chapter 6 (The Ritual of the Soul), Workbook Weeks 1-3

Liturgy vs. Ritual

A Ritual is a repeated action that serves death, the addiction cycle, the grooming behavior, the fantasy pattern. A Liturgy is a repeated action that serves life, prayer, declaration, presence, authority. The core teaching of Chapter 6 is that you cannot simply stop a ritual; you must replace it with a liturgy. You starve the death ritual by establishing a life liturgy in its place. This is how you reclaim authority over your own soul.

Used in context: Chapter 6 (The Ritual of the Soul), Workbook Weeks 3-4, Daily Liturgies throughout

Mother of Shame

The internalized voice of condemnation, unworthiness, and self-rejection. The Mother of Shame is the voice that whispers, "You are dirty. You are broken. You are unlovable. You will never be clean." She shows up in the mirror, in your relationships, in your generational patterns. She is the voice of the culture, the family system, and the enemy, all merged into one condemning presence. Severing ties with the Mother of Shame is the first step of the Spiritual Bill of Divorcement.

Used in context: Chapter 4 (The Art of Leaving), Workbook Week 2 (Days 8-10)

New Creation

The complete spiritual transformation that happens when you surrender your life to Christ. New Creation is not "recovery" or "improvement," it is resurrection. Old things (asa = what you've done) have passed away; all things (bara = what God made you to be) are become new (2 Corinthians 5:17). You are not a recovering addict or a damaged person trying to get better. You are a New Creation walking in a completely transformed identity.

Used in context: Chapter 7 (The Altar of Restoration),

Workbook Week 4 (Day 22), Conclusion

One Flesh, Multiple Histories

The spiritual reality that when two people enter covenant (marriage or sexual union), they merge not just with each other but with all of each other's past partners. You are not just joining with one person; you are joining with their entire relational history. This is the Cumulative Covenant Effect in action. Understanding this is crucial for recognizing why healing past covenants is essential before entering new ones.

Used in context: Chapter 2 (The Mechanics of the Soul), Chapter 3 (The Diagnostic Moment)

Portal

A spiritual opening or gateway created through covenant, sexual union, or agreement. Portals are not metaphorical; they are real spiritual realities. When you enter a sexual covenant, you open a portal between your spirit and the other person's spirit. Through that portal, spiritual influence, demonic oppression, and generational patterns can flow. Closing portals requires severing the covenant and reclaiming your authority. Cleansing portals requires the blood of Jesus.

Used in context: Chapter 2 (The Mechanics of the Soul), Chapter 3 (The Diagnostic Moment), Chapter 7 (The Altar of Restoration), Workbook Weeks 1-4

Shame

The deep belief that you are fundamentally broken, unlovable, and unworthy of restoration. Shame is different from guilt (which says "I did something bad") or conviction (which says "I need to change"). Shame says "I am bad." Shame is the primary weapon the enemy uses to keep you bound. Breaking shame requires understanding that your identity (bara) is separate from your actions (asa), and that the Seventh Man does not condemn, He restores.

Used in context: Chapter 1 (The Con), Chapter 3 (The Diagnostic Moment), Chapter 4 (The Art of Leaving), Workbook Week 1

Seventh Man

Jesus Christ, the only one who can heal the Cumulative Covenant Effect without condemnation. The Seventh Man is the fulfillment of the Woman at the Well narrative, He is the one who sees all of your history (the Five Husbands), knows your present situation (the One), and offers restoration without judgment. He is the only one with the authority and the blood to cleanse your portal and establish you in wholeness. Walking with the Seventh Man is the foundation of all healing.

Used in context: Chapter 3 (The Diagnostic Moment), Chapter 7 (The Altar of Restoration), Workbook Weeks 1-4, throughout all daily practices

Spiritual Bill of Divorcement

A three-step spiritual process for severing ties with unholy covenants and cultural parents: (1) Renounce the agreement, (2) Return the property (emotional baggage, control, false identity), (3) Change your name (establish new identity from the Seventh Man). This is not just emotional processing, it is a formal spiritual act of reclaiming your authority and closing portals. The Bill of Divorcement is performed in the Wilderness season and is essential for moving into cleaving.

Used in context: Chapter 4 (The Art of Leaving), Workbook Week 2 (Days 8-14)

Testimony (Weaponized)

Your personal story of healing and transformation, used as a spiritual weapon to break strongholds and set captives free. Revelation 12:11 says, "They overcame him by the blood of the Lamb, and by the word of their testimony." Your testimony is not just a nice story to share, it is evidence that the enemy's lies are false and that Jesus' power is real. When you walk in your cleansed portal, your very presence becomes weaponized evidence of God's restoration.

Used in context: Chapter 7 (The Altar of Restoration), Workbook Week 4 (Day 24)

The 55s

Cultural and demonic lies planted about sexuality, gender, identity, and worth. The "55s" are the false narratives that the world embeds in your subconscious through media, family systems, and cultural messaging. Examples include: "Your body is currency," "Sex is just recreation," "You are what you look like," "Aging is bankruptcy," "Consent is optional." The 55s are the con, and recognizing them is the first step to freedom.

Used in context: Chapter 1 (The Con), Workbook Week 1 (Day 3)

The Waterpot

The metaphor from John 4 representing what you leave behind at the well, your old identity, your shame, your secrets. The Woman at the Well left her waterpot at the well when she encountered Jesus. The waterpot represents everything you no longer need to carry: the shame, the hiding, the false identity. When you leave your waterpot, you are declaring that you are no longer defined by what you came to get; you are defined by who you've encountered.

Used in context: Chapter 7 (The Altar of Restoration), Workbook Week 4 (Day 23)

Wilderness

The uncomfortable in-between season after you have left (severed ties) but before you have fully cleaved (established new covenant). The Wilderness is not punishment, it is preparation. It is the season where you learn to steward your own soul, where you discover your true frequency, where you practice high-frequency warfare. The Wilderness is disorienting, but it is necessary. God meets you in the Wilderness.

Used in context: Chapter 4 (The Art of Leaving), Workbook

Week 2 (Day 13)

The 7

The number of completion, wholeness, and healing in Scripture. The book uses "the 7" as shorthand for the complete healing journey: seven chapters of teaching, seven steps of deliverance, the Seventh Man (Jesus), the seventh day (rest). The 7 represents the fullness of what God offers, not partial healing, not temporary relief, but complete restoration and wholeness.

Used in context: Throughout the book as a structural and spiritual principle

Use this glossary as your reference guide. When you encounter a term and need clarity, return here. These definitions are not just intellectual; they are the language of your freedom. As you understand these concepts, you begin to speak the language of authority.

The more fluent you become in these terms, the more powerfully you can declare your healing.

APPENDIX C: SMALL GROUP / LEADER GUIDE

Facilitating Sexual Healing in Community

This guide is for pastors, small group leaders, spiritual directors, recovery group facilitators, and anyone called to walk alongside others through the journey of sexual healing. Leading this work is sacred—you are stewarding people's most vulnerable places. This is not just group facilitation; it is spiritual midwifery. You are helping birth freedom.

Before you begin: This material is powerful, and it will provoke spiritual warfare. You cannot lead others through healing you have not pursued yourself. If you have not done your own work around sexual wholeness, generational patterns, and spiritual authority, start there first. You cannot give what you do not have.

1. BEFORE YOU LEAD: LEADER FOUNDATION

How to Prepare Yourself as a Leader

Leading sexual healing work requires three foundations:

1. Personal Healing Work: You must have walked (or be actively walking) your own journey through the 30-day workbook. You don't need to be "perfect," but you do need to be honest about where you are. If you're still in active

addiction or unhealed shame, you are not ready to lead. Seek your own healing first.

2. Spiritual Authority: You must understand your authority in Christ and be comfortable exercising it. This work will provoke demonic resistance, shame attacks, and spiritual opposition. You need to know how to pray with authority, how to close portals, and how to stand in the gap for others. If you are not confident in spiritual warfare, find a mentor or pastor who can train you.

3. Trauma-Informed Awareness: Many participants will carry deep trauma—sexual abuse, assault, betrayal, abandonment. You must understand how trauma lives in the body and the nervous system. Learn the basics of trauma-informed care: recognize freeze/fight/flight responses, understand dissociation, know when to slow down and when to refer to professional counseling.

Practical Preparation:

Complete the 30-day workbook yourself before leading others

Pray daily for spiritual covering over the group

Identify 2-3 trusted counselors/pastors you can refer participants to if needed

Read at least one book on trauma-informed ministry (recommended: The Body Keeps the Score by Bessel van der Kolk, Boundaries by Cloud & Townsend)

Establish your own accountability and support system—you cannot pour from an empty cup

Creating a Safe, Covenant-Protected Space

Safety is not just emotional—it is spiritual. You are creating a space where people will expose their deepest wounds. That space must be protected.

Physical Safety:

Meet in a private, quiet space (not a public coffee shop)

Arrange seating in a circle (no hierarchy, everyone visible)

Have tissues, water, and a Bible available

Ensure confidentiality (what is shared in the group stays in the group)

Spiritual Safety:

Open every meeting with prayer, asking the Holy Spirit to lead and protect

Declare authority over the space: "No spirit of shame, condemnation, or accusation is welcome here. Only the Spirit of Truth."

Close every meeting with a sealing prayer, covering participants as they leave

If you sense demonic oppression during a meeting, pause and pray—do not ignore it

Emotional Safety:

Establish ground rules on Day 1: confidentiality, no cross-talk (responding to others' shares with advice), no judgment

Remind participants they can "pass" on any question or exercise

Normalize discomfort: "This work is hard. It's okay to feel uncomfortable. That's part of the process."

Watch for signs of dissociation or overwhelm—if someone "checks out," gently bring them back or offer a break

Understanding Trauma-Informed Facilitation

Trauma-informed facilitation means recognizing that many participants are carrying wounds that affect how they process information, relate to authority, and experience safety.

Key Principles:

Safety First — Always prioritize emotional and spiritual safety over "getting through the material."

Choice — Give participants control over their participation (they can pass, take breaks, leave if needed)

Collaboration — You are not the expert on their healing; you are a guide walking alongside them

Empowerment — The goal is to help them reclaim authority, not to create dependence on you

Trustworthiness — Be consistent, keep your word, maintain boundaries

Recognizing Trauma Responses:

Fight: Anger, defensiveness, challenging your authority

Flight: Wanting to leave, avoiding eye contact, changing the subject

Freeze: Shutting down, going silent, dissociating (glazed eyes, flat affect)

Fawn: Over-apologizing, people-pleasing, trying to "be good."

How to Respond:

Slow down, lower your voice, create space

Validate their experience: "It makes sense that this is hard. You're safe here."

Offer choice: "Would you like to take a break? Would you like to pass on this question?"

Do not force disclosure or push through resistance—trauma cannot be rushed

Managing Disclosure and Boundaries

Participants will share deeply personal, often painful stories. You must hold these stories with care while maintaining healthy boundaries.

What to Do:

Listen without judgment or shock

Validate their courage: "Thank you for trusting us with this."

Remind them they are not alone: "You are not the only one

who has walked this road."

Pray for them (ask permission first)

What NOT to Do:

Do not give advice or try to "fix" them

Do not share your own story in response (this is their time, not yours)

Do not minimize their pain ("At least it wasn't worse" or "God works all things for good")

Do not pressure them to forgive or "move on" before they're ready

When to Refer: If someone discloses active suicidal ideation, ongoing abuse, or a severe mental health crisis, refer them to professional help immediately. You are a spiritual guide, not a therapist. Know your limits.

2. FACILITATING THE 7-CHAPTER TEACHING ARC

Each chapter builds on the previous one. Do not skip chapters or rush through the material. The teaching arc is designed to move participants from awareness (The Con) to diagnosis (The Woman at the Well) to liberation (The Art of Leaving) to restoration (The Altar).

Suggested Pace:

Option 1: One chapter per week (7 weeks total), then begin the 30-day workbook

Option 2: Two chapters per week (3.5 weeks), then begin the 30-day workbook

Option 3: Read all 7 chapters individually, then gather weekly to discuss + work through the 30-day workbook together

Sample Discussion Questions by Chapter

Chapter 1: The Con

Which "55" (cultural lie) resonates most with your experience? How has it shaped your view of sexuality or identity?

How have you seen the "gendered traps" (men taught to conquer, women taught to perform) play out in your life or relationships?

What does it mean to you that sexual sin is not just "moral failure" but spiritual mechanics? How does that change your understanding of healing?

Chapter 2: The Mechanics of the Soul

How does the distinction between asa (what you've done) and bara (what God made you to be) shift your understanding of shame?

What does "one flesh, multiple histories" mean for your current or future relationships?

Have you experienced the Cumulative Covenant Effect—feeling like past relationships are still affecting your present? How?

Chapter 3: The Diagnostic Moment

Who are your "Five Husbands" (past covenants/entanglements)? (Note: This is optional disclosure—participants can journal privately if they're not ready to share.)

How does the Woman at the Well's story mirror your own journey? Where do you see yourself in the narrative?

What does it mean to you that the Seventh Man (Jesus) doesn't condemn but restores?

Chapter 4: The Art of Leaving

Which "cultural parent" (Mother of Shame, Father of Lust, Ancestral Altar) has the strongest hold on you?

What does it look like for you to perform a Spiritual Bill of Divorcement—renouncing, returning, and changing your name?

How do you feel about the Wilderness season? What makes it uncomfortable? What makes it necessary?

Chapter 5: The Power of Cleaving

What does "Dabeq Frequency" (spiritual fusion in covenant) look like in a healthy relationship?

How do you discern whether someone is at your frequency or

whether you're settling for less?

What generational patterns do you want to break so your children inherit blessing instead of curse?

Chapter 6: The Ritual of the Soul

What is your personal addiction cycle? Can you identify the four stages (Fantasy, Engagement, Amplification, Acting Out)?

What does it look like to interrupt the fantasy at Stage 2? What Life Liturgy could you establish to replace the death ritual?

How do you practice high-frequency warfare in your daily life?

Chapter 7: The Altar of Restoration

What is your "waterpot"—the thing you're ready to leave behind at the well?

How has your healing journey become (or how could it become) weaponized testimony that sets others free?

What does it mean to walk as a New Creation, not just a "recovering" person?

How to Create Space for Personal Application Without Forcing Disclosure?

Not everyone will be ready to share their story publicly. Honor that.

Strategies:

Offer journaling time during the meeting (10-15 minutes of silent reflection)

Use the phrase "You can share as much or as little as you're comfortable with"

Model vulnerability yourself, but don't dominate the conversation

Remind participants they can process privately and bring questions to you later

Normalize silence—not everyone needs to speak every week

Managing Different Perspectives and Resistance

Some participants will resist the teaching, especially around spiritual warfare, generational habits, or the mechanics of covenant. This is normal.

How to Respond:

Acknowledge their perspective: "I hear you. This is challenging material."

Invite curiosity: "What if this were true? How would that change things?"

Don't argue or defend—let the Holy Spirit do the convincing

Offer grace: "You don't have to agree with everything. Take

what resonates and leave the rest."

If resistance becomes disruptive, address it privately after the meeting

3. LEADING THE 30-DAY WORKBOOK IN COMMUNITY

The 30-day workbook is designed for individual daily practice, but it can be powerfully supported by weekly community gatherings.

Two Options:

Option 1: Individual Daily Work + Weekly GatheringParticipants complete the daily practices on their own (5-20 minutes per day) and gather weekly to process, share, and support each other. This is the recommended model.

Weekly Gathering Structure (120 minutes):

Week 1 Gathering: Discuss Days 1-7 (The Inventory)

Week 2 Gathering: Discuss Days 8-14 (The Liberation)

Week 3 Gathering: Discuss Days 15-21 (The Restoration)

Week 4 Gathering: Discuss Days 22-30 (The Ascension)

Option 2: Structured Group PaceThe group works through the 30-day workbook together, completing one day's practice during each meeting. This requires 30 meetings (or condensing to 2-3 days per meeting). This is more intensive and requires significant time commitment.

How to Structure Weekly Group Meetings (120-Minute Model)

Opening / Centering (15 minutes)

Welcome and check-in: "How are you feeling as you enter this space today?"

Opening prayer: Invite the Holy Spirit, declare authority over the space, ask for protection and revelation

Grounding exercise: Deep breathing, centering prayer, or brief Scripture reading

Teaching / Discussion (40 minutes)

Review the week's theme (e.g., Week 1: The Inventory)

Discuss 2-3 key days from the week's practices

Sample questions:

"What was the hardest day this week? Why?"

"What did you discover about yourself?"

"Where did you feel resistance? Where did you feel breakthrough?"

Allow space for participants to share (but don't force it)

Frequency Work / Spiritual Practice (20 minutes)

Lead the group through one of the week's Frequency Work exercises together

Example: Week 2, Day 14 (The Frequency of Freedom)—practice feeling the shift from shame to freedom as a group

This is not just intellectual—guide them to feel the spiritual vibration shift

Play instrumental worship music softly in the background if helpful

Testimony / Witness (15 minutes)

Invite 1-2 participants to share a breakthrough, insight, or struggle from the week

Remind the group: "Your story is not just personal—it's a weapon. When you share, you're breaking strongholds for others."

Pray for those who share

Closing / Authority Declarations (10 minutes)

Lead the group in one of the week's Authority Declarations (speak aloud together)

Example: Week 3, Day 21—"I have authority over my own

soul. I am the steward. I am free."

Closing prayer: Seal the work done, cover participants as they leave, declare protection over the week ahead

Remind participants of the daily practices for the coming week

How to Honor the Frequency Work / Spiritual Dimensions

This is not just a Bible study or a recovery group—it is spiritual warfare and frequency shifting. You must create space for the felt experience of healing, not just the intellectual understanding.

Practical Tips:

Dim the lights slightly during Frequency Work (creates a contemplative atmosphere)

Use instrumental worship music to help participants "feel" the shift

Guide them with language like: "Notice what you feel in your body. Where is the tension? Where is the peace?"

Normalize the discomfort: "If this feels awkward, that's okay. We're learning a new language."

Do not rush this section—it is the most important part of the meeting

Managing the Vulnerable Moments (Especially Weeks 2-3)

Week 2 (The Liberation) and Week 3 (The Restoration) are the most intense. Participants are severing ties, confronting triggers, and starving rituals. Expect tears, anger, and breakthroughs.

How to Hold Space:

Slow down—do not rush through the material

Validate emotions: "It's okay to cry. It's okay to be angry. This is hard work."

Offer breaks if needed

Have tissues and water readily available

Pray over participants who are struggling (ask permission first)

Remind them: "The Wilderness is not punishment—it's preparation. God is with you here."

4. ESSENTIAL LEADER SKILLS

Creating Psychological and Spiritual Safety

Safety is the foundation of healing. Without it, participants will not open up, and the work will remain surface-level.

How to Create Safety:

Be consistent (same time, same place, same structure)

Be trustworthy (keep confidentiality, follow through on commitments)

Be non-judgmental (no shock, no condemnation, no fixing)

Be present (put away your phone, make eye contact, listen deeply)

Be humble (admit when you don't know something, ask for help when needed)

Holding Space for the Wilderness Season

The Wilderness (Week 2) is disorienting and uncomfortable. Participants will want to quit, go back, or numb out. Your job is to hold steady and remind them that the Wilderness is necessary.

What to Say:

"The Wilderness is not punishment—it's preparation."

"You're not lost—you're being led."

"The discomfort means you're healing, not failing."

"God meets you in the Wilderness. He always has."

What NOT to Say:

"Just push through it."

"It's not that bad."

"You should be grateful for this process."

Recognizing and Responding to Trauma Responses

If someone dissociates (glazed eyes, flat affect, unresponsive), stop and bring them back gently.

How to Respond:

Lower your voice, slow your pace

Say their name gently: "Sarah, can you hear me? You're safe. You're here with us."

Ask them to notice their surroundings: "Can you name three things you see in this room?"

Offer a break: "Would you like to step outside for a moment?"

Do not force them to continue—trauma cannot be rushed

When to Refer to Counseling / Professional Support

You are not a therapist. Know your limits.

Refer to professional help if:

Someone discloses active suicidal ideation or self-harm

Someone discloses ongoing abuse (physical, sexual, emotional)

Someone is experiencing severe mental health crisis (psychosis, dissociation, panic attacks)

Someone's trauma is too complex for a group setting (requires individual therapy)

How to Refer:

Be direct and compassionate: "I care about you, and I think you need more support than I can provide in this setting. I'd like to connect you with a counselor who specializes in trauma."

Have a list of 2-3 trusted counselors ready to share

Follow up with them after the referral to ensure they connected

Managing Disclosure in Community

When someone shares a deeply personal story, the group may not know how to respond. Guide them.

What to Do:

Thank the person for their courage: "Thank you for trusting us with this."

Invite the group to hold space: "Let's just sit with this for a moment. No need to respond or fix."

Pray for the person (ask permission first)

Remind the group of confidentiality

What NOT to Do:

Do not allow cross-talk (other participants responding with advice or their own stories)

Do not minimize or spiritualize their pain ("God works all things for good")

Do not pressure them to forgive or "move on"

5. GROUP DYNAMICS & CHALLENGES

How to Handle Resistance and Defense Mechanisms

Resistance is normal. It is the soul's way of protecting itself from pain.

Common Forms of Resistance:

Intellectualizing (staying in the head, avoiding feelings)

Minimizing ("It wasn't that bad")

Deflecting (changing the subject, making jokes)

Blaming (focusing on others' faults instead of their own)

How to Respond:

Name it gently: "I notice you're staying in your head. What would it be like to drop into your heart for a moment?"

Invite curiosity: "What are you protecting yourself from right now?"

Do not force—resistance is information, not defiance

Managing Shame in the Group Setting

Shame thrives in secrecy and isolation. The group setting can be powerfully healing—or deeply triggering.

How to Manage Shame:

Normalize it: "Shame is part of the journey. Everyone here has felt it."

Name it: "That voice telling you you're too broken to be healed? That's the Mother of Shame. She's a liar."

Counter it with truth: "You are not what you've done. You are what God made you to be."

Invite testimony: "Has anyone else felt this way?" (This breaks the isolation.)

Supporting Both Married and Single Participants

This material applies to both married and single people, but the application looks different.

For Married Participants:

Focus on healing past covenants, establishing Dabeq Frequency, and creating generational blessings

Address how to navigate healing while in a relationship (communication, boundaries, patience)

For Single Participants:

Focus on healing past covenants, stewarding the Wilderness season, and preparing for future covenant

Address the temptation to rush into relationship before healing is complete

Do not create hierarchy (married people are not "more healed" than single people). Both are on the same journey.

Navigating Different Healing Timelines

Some participants will move quickly through the material. Others will need to repeat weeks or take breaks. Honor both.

What to Say:

"Healing is not linear. There is no 'right' timeline."

"If you need to repeat a week, do it. If you need to take a break, take it."

"You are not behind. You are exactly where you need to be."

Addressing Spiritual Warfare and Demonization Questions

Some participants will ask: "Am I demonized? Do I need deliverance?"

How to Respond:

Affirm the reality of spiritual warfare: "Yes, the enemy is real, and he does oppress believers."

Clarify the difference between oppression and possession: "If you are a believer, you cannot be possessed. But you can be oppressed through open portals."

Offer practical steps: "The 30-day workbook is a form of deliverance. You are closing portals and reclaiming authority."

If someone needs more intensive deliverance ministry, refer them to a pastor or deliverance minister trained in this work

6. PRAYER & SPIRITUAL AUTHORITY FOR LEADERS

Prayers Leaders Should Pray Before and During Groups

Before the Meeting (Leader's Personal Prayer):

"Father, I come before You as a steward of this sacred space. I ask for Your wisdom, Your discernment, and Your protection. Cover me with the blood of Jesus. Give me eyes to see what You see and ears to hear what You're saying. I declare authority over this space—no spirit of shame, condemnation, or accusation is welcome here. Only the Spirit of Truth. I surrender this meeting to You. Lead me. Use me. Protect those who will gather. In Jesus' name, Amen."

Opening Prayer (With the Group):

"Holy Spirit, we invite You into this space. We declare that You are Lord here. We ask for Your protection, Your revelation, and Your healing power. We renounce every lie of the enemy. We close every portal that has been opened through shame, lust, or broken covenant. We declare this to be holy ground. Meet us here. In Jesus' name, Amen."

Closing Prayer (With the Group):

"Father, we thank You for the work You've done in this space tonight. We seal it with the blood of Jesus. We cover each person as they leave, protect their minds, their hearts, their homes. We declare that no weapon formed against them will prosper. We release them into Your care. In Jesus' name, Amen."

How to Spiritually Cover the Group Space

Before each meeting, walk the room and pray over it. Declare authority over the space. Anoint the room with oil if you feel led. This is not superstition, it is spiritual stewardship.

What to Pray:

"I declare this space is covered by the blood of Jesus."

"No demonic presence is welcome here."

"I bind every spirit of shame, lust, condemnation, and accusation."

"I invite the Holy Spirit to fill this space and lead this meeting."

Managing Resistance and Demonic Opposition

You will encounter spiritual resistance. Participants may feel sudden anxiety, anger, or the urge to quit. This is not coincidence, it is warfare.

How to Respond:

Recognize it: "I sense some spiritual resistance in the room. Let's pause and pray."

Pray aloud: "In the name of Jesus, I bind every spirit of fear, shame, and confusion. You have no authority here. Leave now."

Invite participants to declare authority: "Let's all say together: 'I have authority in Christ. I am not afraid.'"

Do not ignore it, address it directly and move forward

Maintaining the Altar as a Leader

You cannot lead others to the altar if you are not maintaining your own. Daily restoration is not optional for leaders.

Daily Practices for Leaders:

Pray for each participant by name

Read Scripture and declare authority over your own soul

Practice the Frequency Work yourself

Stay connected to your own support system

Take breaks when needed, you cannot pour from an empty cup

7. RED FLAGS & BOUNDARY MANAGEMENT

Signs Someone May Need Individual Counseling Instead of Group

Active suicidal ideation or self-harm

Severe dissociation or flashbacks

Ongoing abuse (they are not safe to process in a group setting)

Dominating the group (taking up all the airtime, making it about them)

Severe mental health crisis (psychosis, mania, severe depression)

How to Address:

Speak to them privately after the meeting

Be direct and compassionate: "I care about you, and I think you need more support than this group can provide. Let me connect you with a counselor."

Do not shame them, frame it as care, not rejection

How to Handle Disclosure of Abuse or Trauma

If someone discloses abuse, do not minimize or spiritualize it.

What to Do:

Validate: "I'm so sorry that happened to you. That was not your fault."

Offer support: "Thank you for trusting us with this. You are not alone."

Refer if needed: "I'd like to connect you with a counselor who specializes in trauma."

Pray for them (ask permission first)

What NOT to Do:

Do not ask for details (this is not an investigation)

Do not say "God works all things for good" (this minimizes their pain)

Do not pressure them to forgive their abuser

Managing Transference and Intensity

Participants may develop strong emotional attachments to you as the leader. This is called transference, and it is normal in healing work.

How to Manage:

Maintain clear boundaries (no private meetings alone, no

texting outside of group logistics)

Redirect them to the Seventh Man: "I'm honored you trust me, but Jesus is the Healer, not me."

If transference becomes inappropriate (romantic feelings, dependency), address it directly and refer them to individual counseling

Protecting the Group from Disruption

If one participant is dominating the group, derailing discussions, or creating an unsafe environment, you must address it.

How to Address:

Speak to them privately after the meeting

Be direct: "I've noticed you're taking up a lot of airtime. I need to make sure everyone has space to share."

Set boundaries: "I need you to limit your sharing to 3-5 minutes so others can participate."

If they cannot respect boundaries, ask them to leave the group (this is rare, but necessary to protect the group)

8. AFTER THE JOURNEY: TRANSITIONING TO DAILY RESTORATION

Ongoing Community and Accountability Structures

After the 30-day workbook, participants need ongoing support to maintain the altar.

Options:

Monthly check-in meetings (60 minutes)

Accountability partnerships (2-3 people meeting weekly)

Online group chat for daily encouragement

Annual "refresher" groups (repeating the 30-day workbook)

Leadership Development: Graduates Becoming Leaders

The best leaders are those who have walked the journey themselves. Invite graduates to co-lead future groups.

How to Develop Leaders:

Invite them to observe a group before leading

Have them co-facilitate with you (leading one section of the meeting)

Provide ongoing training and support

Pray over them and commission them as leaders

Resource List for Continued Support

Provide participants with a list of resources for continued healing:

Recommended books (theology, trauma, sexuality)

Counselors and therapists (trauma-informed, Christian)

Ministries and organizations (sexual healing, deliverance, recovery)

Online communities and support groups

9. SAMPLE OPENING & CLOSING PRAYERS

Opening Prayer (Week 1: The Inventory):

"Father, we come before You with open hearts and willing spirits. We are ready to see the truth, about ourselves, about our history, about the covenants we've made. Give us courage to name what needs to be healed. Holy Spirit, lead us into all truth. We trust You. In Jesus' name, Amen."

Closing Prayer (Week 2: The Liberation):

"Father, we thank You for the work of liberation You've begun in us. We have renounced the Mother of Shame, the Father of Lust, and the Ancestral Altar. We have severed ties. We have changed our names. Now we ask You to seal this work.

Cover us as we walk through the Wilderness. Remind us that You are with us. We are not alone. In Jesus' name, Amen."

Opening Prayer (Week 3: The Restoration):

"Father, we are learning to interrupt the fantasy, to starve the ritual, and to establish new rhythms. This is hard work, and we need Your strength. Give us the authority to reclaim our own souls. Teach us to walk in dominion, not in need. We are ready to be free. In Jesus' name, Amen."

Closing Prayer (Week 4: The Ascension):

"Father, we stand before You as New Creations. Old things have passed away. All things are become new. We are not recovering, we are transformed. We are not victims, we are victors. We are not broken, we are whole. Seal this work. Establish us in our authority. Use our stories to set others free. We are Yours. In Jesus' name, Amen."

10. LEADER COVENANT

As a leader of this work, I commit to:

Walk my own healing journey — I will not lead others where I have not gone myself.

Maintain spiritual authority — I will pray daily, declare authority over the group space, and stand against spiritual opposition.

Create safety — I will protect confidentiality, honor boundaries, and create a space where people can be vulnerable without fear.

Stay trauma-informed — I will recognize trauma responses, slow down when needed, and refer to professional help when appropriate.

Point to the Seventh Man — I will not position myself as the healer; I will point participants to Jesus as the source of all healing.

Maintain boundaries — I will not meet privately with participants alone, engage in inappropriate relationships, or allow transference to go unaddressed.

Care for myself — I will maintain my own altar, stay connected to my support system, and take breaks when needed.

Honor the process — I will not rush participants, force disclosure, or pressure them to "move on" before they're ready.

Steward the testimony — I will honor the stories shared in this space and use them (with permission) to encourage others.

Walk in humility — I will admit when I don't know something, ask for help when needed, and remain teachable.

I understand that leading this work is sacred, and I commit to stewarding it with integrity, compassion, and authority.

You are not just facilitating a group—you are midwifing freedom. This is holy work. Walk in your authority. Trust the Seventh Man. He will meet you here.

Every single time.

APPENDIX D: AUTHORITY DECLARATIONS QUICK REFERENCE

Speaking Truth Over Your Soul

HOW TO USE THIS REFERENCE?

These are not affirmations. Affirmations are positive thoughts you repeat to yourself in hopes they'll become true. Authority Declarations are statements of truth you speak aloud to shift the spiritual atmosphere and reclaim dominion over your own soul.

The difference is critical: affirmations come from need; declarations come from authority.

When you speak these declarations, you are not trying to convince yourself of something you hope is true. You are announcing what is already true in the spiritual realm and commanding your soul, your mind, and the atmosphere around you to align with that truth.

How to Use These Declarations?

Print them and post them where you'll see them daily — bathroom mirror, car dashboard, phone lock screen, journal cover

Speak them aloud — declarations have no power if they stay in your head; they must be spoken into the atmosphere

Choose one declaration per day — return to it throughout the day, especially when triggered or under attack

Use them in high-frequency warfare — when shame attacks, when lust tempts, when the enemy whispers lies, speak these declarations with authority

Memorize the ones that resonate most — let them become your new internal soundtrack, replacing the "55s"

Declare them over your children and lineage — these are generational declarations; speak them over your descendants

Remember: You are not begging God to make these things true. You are declaring what He has already established. You are speaking from victory, not toward it.

1. OVER SHAME

"I am not what I've done. I am what God made me to be."

Context: Use this when the Mother of Shame whispers that your past defines you. Asa (what you've done) does not determine bara (what God created you to be).

"Shame has no voice in my life. I silence her now."

Context: Speak this when you hear the condemning voice of unworthiness. You have authority to silence the Mother of Shame.

"I am beloved, chosen, and whole."

Context: Counter the lie that you are broken beyond repair. Your identity is rooted in God's love, not your history.

"The Seventh Man does not condemn me. I do not condemn myself."

Context: When shame tries to convince you that God is disappointed or disgusted, remember: Jesus came to restore, not condemn.

"I am not dirty. I am not damaged. I am sanctified."

Context: Use this when shame attacks your sense of purity or worth. The blood of Jesus has cleansed you completely.

"My scars are proof of healing, not evidence of failure."

Context: When you're tempted to hide your history, remember: your scars are your testimony. They are weaponized evidence.

"I refuse to carry what was never mine to carry."

Context: Speak this when you're tempted to take on shame that belongs to someone else—an abuser, a parent, a past partner.

"I am not too broken to be healed. I am not too far gone to be restored."

Context: When hopelessness whispers that you're beyond redemption, declare this truth: no one is too broken for the Seventh Man.

"Shame is a liar. Truth is my foundation."

Context: Simple, direct, powerful. Use this as a daily reset when shame tries to creep back in.

"I walk in the light. I have nothing to hide."

Context: When shame tries to keep you in secrecy and isolation, declare this: you are no longer hiding. You are walking in freedom.

2. OVER LUST & SEXUAL TEMPTATION

"I have authority over my own mind. I decide what I feed."

Context: Use this at Stage 2 of the addiction cycle (Engagement) when the fantasy begins. You have the authority to interrupt it.

"I am not a slave to lust. I am free."

Context: When lust tries to convince you that you're powerless, declare this: you are not in bondage. You are free in Christ.

"I cast down every imagination that exalts itself against the knowledge of God."

Context: This is 2 Corinthians 10:5 in action. Speak this when the fantasy begins to build. You have the authority to cast it down.

"I starve the ritual. I feed the liturgy."

Context: When you're tempted to return to the death ritual, remind yourself: you are establishing a new pattern. You are replacing, not just resisting.

"My body is a temple. I steward it with honor."

Context: When lust tries to reduce your body to an object or a tool, declare this: your body is sacred, and you are its steward.

"I interrupt the fantasy. I choose truth."

Context: Simple and direct. Use this the moment the fantasy begins. Interrupt it immediately and replace it with truth.

"Lust has no claim on me. I belong to the Seventh Man."

Context: When lust tries to convince you that you "need" it or that it's part of your identity, declare this: you belong to Jesus, not to lust.

"I am not defined by my desires. I am defined by my covenant."

Context: When desire feels overwhelming, remember: your identity is not rooted in what you want; it's rooted in who you belong to.

"I choose the high frequency. I reject the counterfeit."

Context: When temptation presents itself as "relief" or "comfort," declare this: you are choosing the real thing, not the counterfeit.

"I am a warrior, not a victim. I fight from victory, not toward it."

Context: When you feel weak or powerless in the face of temptation, remember: you are not fighting for victory. You are fighting from victory.

3. OVER PAST COVENANTS (THE FIVE HUSBANDS)

"I renounce every unholy covenant I have made."

Context: Use this as part of your Spiritual Bill of Divorcement. Speak the names of past partners (aloud or in your heart) and renounce the covenant.

"I reclaim what was stolen. I return what was never mine."

Context: When you're doing the work of returning emotional baggage and reclaiming your authority, declare this: you are taking back what belongs to you.

"The Five have no legal standing. I sever every tie."

Context: When past relationships try to exert influence over your present, declare this: they have no authority. You are severing the ties.

"I am no longer bound to my past. I am free."

Context: Simple and powerful. Use this when memories or regrets try to pull you back into old patterns.

"I close every portal that was opened through broken covenant."

Context: When you sense spiritual oppression or demonic influence from past relationships, declare this: you are closing the portals.

"I am not defined by who I've been with. I am defined by who I belong to."

Context: When shame tries to reduce your identity to your sexual history, declare this: your identity is rooted in the Seventh Man, not your past.

"I release every person I've been entangled with. I set them free, and I am free."

Context: Use this when you're tempted to hold onto bitterness, resentment, or attachment to past partners. Release them and release yourself.

"The Cumulative Covenant Effect is broken. I am whole."

Context: When you feel the weight of multiple past relationships affecting your present, declare this: the cycle is broken. You are whole.

"I am no longer carrying the Five. I am walking with the Seventh Man."

Context: Powerful declaration for the transition from bondage to freedom. You are no longer defined by the Five; you are walking with the One who heals.

"My history is sanctified. My portal is cleansed."

Context: When shame tries to convince you that your past disqualifies you, declare this: God has sanctified your history.

Your portal is cleansed.

4. OVER GENERATIONAL PATTERNS

"The cycle stops with me. I am a healer, not a curse-carrier."

Context: When you recognize generational patterns repeating in your life, declare this: you are breaking the cycle. You are not passing it on.

"I renounce every generational habit. I establish generational blessing."

Context: Use this when you're doing the work of severing ties with the Ancestral Altar. You are not just breaking curses; you are establishing blessing.

"My children will inherit wholeness, not brokenness."

Context: When you're tempted to believe that your past will doom your children, declare this: your healing changes their inheritance.

"I am not my parents. I am not my ancestors. I am a New Creation."

Context: When you feel the weight of family dysfunction or inherited trauma, declare this: you are not bound to repeat their patterns.

"I refuse to carry what my ancestors chose. I set it down."

Context: Simple and direct. Use this when you recognize that you're carrying generational baggage that was never yours to carry.

"I open a portal of blessing for my lineage. The curse is broken."

Context: When you're ready to shift from breaking curses to establishing blessing, declare this: you are opening a new portal for your descendants.

"My healing is not just personal. It is generational."

Context: When you're tempted to minimize the importance of your healing journey, remember: this is bigger than you. Your healing changes your lineage.

"I am a portal of life, not death. My children will walk in freedom."

Context: Powerful declaration for parents. You are not passing on dysfunction; you are establishing a new legacy.

"The Ancestral Altar is dismantled. I build a new altar of restoration."

Context: When you're ready to move from severing ties to establishing new patterns, declare this: the old altar is gone. You are building a new one.

"I am the generation that breaks the cycle. I am the generation that heals."

Context: When you need courage to do the hard work of generational healing, declare this: you are the one. The cycle stops with you.

5. FOR NEW CREATION IDENTITY

"I am a New Creation. Old things have passed away; all things are become new."

Context: This is 2 Corinthians 5:17. Use this daily to remind yourself: you are not recovering. You are transformed.

"I am not a recovering addict. I am a New Creation walking in freedom."

Context: When the world tries to define you by your past struggle, declare this: you are not defined by what you're recovering from. You are defined by who you are in Christ.

"I am whole. I am holy. I am free."

Context: Simple, powerful, daily declaration. Speak this over yourself every morning.

"I am not broken. I am being made whole."

Context: When you're in the middle of the healing process and it feels messy, declare this: you are not broken. You are in process.

"I am not my history. I am my destiny."

Context: When shame tries to convince you that your past determines your future, declare this: your destiny is not your history.

"I am beloved. I am chosen. I am His."

Context: When you need to remember your core identity, declare this: you are not defined by what you've done. You are defined by whose you are.

"I am not what the enemy says I am. I am what God says I am."

Context: When lies and accusations come, declare this: the enemy's voice has no authority. God's voice is the only one that matters.

"I am sanctified, justified, and glorified."

Context: Theological declaration grounded in Romans 8:30. You are not waiting to be made whole; you already are.

"I am a temple of the Holy Spirit. I am sacred ground."

Context: When you're tempted to treat your body or soul carelessly, declare this: you are sacred. You are holy ground.

"I am not going back. I am moving forward as a New Creation."

Context: When the enemy tries to pull you back into old

patterns, declare this: you are not going back. You are moving forward.

6. FOR AUTHORITY & DOMINION

"I have authority over my own soul. I am the steward."

Context: Core declaration of dominion. Use this when you need to reclaim authority over your thoughts, emotions, and choices.

"No weapon formed against me will prosper. Every tongue that rises against me in judgment, I condemn."

Context: This is Isaiah 54:17. Use this when under spiritual attack or when lies and accusations come against you.

"I am not a victim. I am a victor."

Context: When you're tempted to see yourself as powerless or defeated, declare this: you are not a victim. You are victorious in Christ.

"I bind every spirit of shame, lust, and condemnation. You have no authority here."

Context: Use this in high-frequency warfare when you sense demonic oppression. You have the authority to bind the enemy.

"I loose the Spirit of Truth, the Spirit of Freedom, and the Spirit of Wholeness over my life."

Context: After binding the enemy, loose the Holy Spirit. You have the authority to bind and loose (Matthew 16:19).

"I am not going back. My authority is sealed."

Context: Simple, direct, powerful. Use this when the enemy tries to convince you that you'll fall back into old patterns.

"I walk in dominion, not in need. I speak from authority, not from desperation."

Context: When you're tempted to pray from a place of begging or pleading, declare this: you are speaking from authority, not need.

"Greater is He that is in me than he that is in the world."

Context: This is 1 John 4:4. Use this when you feel overwhelmed by the enemy's attacks. The Spirit in you is greater.

"I have the mind of Christ. I think His thoughts. I speak His truth."

Context: When your thoughts are chaotic or under attack, declare this: you have the mind of Christ (1 Corinthians 2:16).

"I am seated with Christ in heavenly places. I am above, not beneath."

Context: This is Ephesians 2:6. Use this when you need to remember your position: you are seated with Christ, far above all principalities and powers.

"I reclaim every inch of ground the enemy has stolen. I take back what is mine."

Context: When you're ready to move from defense to offense, declare this: you are reclaiming territory.

"I am a warrior. I am a priest. I am a king."

Context: Powerful identity declaration. You are not just a survivor; you are royalty and you are called to fight.

7. FOR COVENANT & CLEAVING

"I establish the Dabeq Frequency. We are one flesh, fused in covenant."

Context: For married couples establishing spiritual fusion. Speak this over your marriage.

"My portal is cleansed. I am ready for covenant."

Context: For singles preparing for marriage. Declare this when you've done the healing work and you're ready to enter covenant.

"We are not codependent. We are powerfully aligned."

Context: For couples who are learning the difference between unhealthy enmeshment and healthy cleaving.

"I am a source, not a drain. I bring life to this covenant."

Context: For those who have completed the Courtship of Self and are ready to enter the Courtship of Frequency.

"The Third Cord is woven into our covenant. The Seventh Man is in our marriage bed."

Context: For married couples inviting Jesus into the center of their covenant. This is Ecclesiastes 4:12 in action.

"I am not settling. I am waiting for my frequency."

Context: For singles who are tempted to settle for someone who is not at their frequency. Declare this and wait.

"My children will inherit the Dabeq Frequency. I am establishing a new legacy."

Context: For parents who are establishing covenant and want their children to inherit wholeness, not brokenness.

"I am sealed in covenant. I am protected. I am whole."

Context: For married people who need to remember the power and protection of covenant.

8. FOR SPIRITUAL WARFARE

"I cast down every imagination that exalts itself against the knowledge of God."

Context: This is 2 Corinthians 10:5. Use this when lies, fantasies, or accusations come. You have the authority to cast them down.

"Truth vibrates in my atmosphere. Lies have no place here."

Context: Use this in high-frequency warfare to shift the spiritual atmosphere around you.

"I am a warrior, not a worrier. I fight from victory, not toward it."

Context: When anxiety or fear tries to take hold, declare this: you are not fighting for victory. You are fighting from victory.

"I speak life, not death. I declare truth, not lies."

Context: When you're tempted to speak negatively over yourself or your situation, declare this: you have the authority to speak life.

"I am covered by the blood of Jesus. No weapon formed against me will prosper."

Context: Daily declaration of protection. Speak this over yourself every morning.

"I resist the devil, and he flees from me."

Context: This is James 4:7. Use this when under direct spiritual attack. You have the authority to resist, and the enemy must flee.

"I am not afraid. I am not intimidated. I am not backing down."

Context: When the enemy tries to use fear or intimidation to silence you, declare this: you are not afraid.

"I am a threat to the kingdom of darkness. My freedom is a weapon."

Context: When you need to remember the power of your testimony and your healing, declare this: your freedom is a weapon.

"I shift the frequency. I change the atmosphere. I declare truth."

Context: Use this when you walk into a room or situation that feels heavy or oppressive. You have the authority to shift the frequency.

"I am not under attack. I am on the offensive. I am taking ground."

Context: When you're ready to move from defense to offense, declare this: you are not just defending. You are advancing.

9. FOR DAILY RESTORATION

"I am not going back."

Context: Simple, direct, daily declaration. Speak this every morning to remind yourself: you are moving forward, not backward.

"My authority is sealed. My portal is cleansed. I am free."

Context: Daily declaration of your position. Use this to remind yourself of the work you've done and the authority you walk in.

"I am His. I am whole. I am loved."

Context: Simple, powerful, daily reminder of your identity.

"I maintain the altar. I walk in daily restoration."

Context: Use this to remind yourself that healing is not a one-time event. It's a daily practice.

"I am a New Creation. Today, I walk in that truth."

Context: Daily declaration of identity. Speak this every morning to set the tone for the day.

"I choose freedom. I choose truth. I choose the Seventh Man."

Context: Daily declaration of choice. You are not a victim of circumstance; you are making a choice every day.

"I am not alone. The Seventh Man walks with me."

Context: When you feel isolated or overwhelmed, declare this: you are not alone. Jesus is with you.

"I am grateful. I am free. I am His."

Context: Simple daily declaration of gratitude and identity.

10. DECLARATIONS BY SEASON

FOR THE WILDERNESS SEASON:

"The Wilderness is not punishment. It is preparation. God meets me here."

Context: When you're in the uncomfortable in-between season after leaving but before cleaving, declare this: the Wilderness is necessary.

FOR THE RESTORATION SEASON:

"I am breaking the cycle at the root. I am establishing new rhythms."

Context: When you're in the hard work of interrupting rituals and establishing liturgies, declare this: you are doing the work.

FOR THE ASCENSION SEASON:

"I am a New Creation. I walk as a portal of blessing. My testimony is a weapon."

Context: When you're ready to step into your full authority and use your story to set others free, declare this: you are ascending.

Print these declarations. Speak them aloud. Let them become

your new internal soundtrack.

You are not begging. You are declaring.

You are not hoping. You are commanding.

You are not recovering. You are reigning.

This is your authority. Walk in it.

www.ingramcontent.com/pod-product-compliance
Lightning Source LLC
LaVergne TN
LVHW031342150826
845673LV00009B/2824

* 9 7 9 8 9 0 4 1 7 0 1 1 0 *